15.96
S.O.
G.K. Hall

DATE DUE			

Thomas Parnell

Twayne's English Authors Series

Bertram H. Davis, Editor

Florida State University

TEAS 397

Engraved by W. Hopwood, from an Original of Sr. Godfrey Kneller.

PARNELL.

Printed for C.Cooke, 17, Paternoster Row, October 21, 1796.

THOMAS PARNELL
(1679–1718)
Engraving by W. Hopwood, 1796,
from non-extant original of Sir Godfrey Kneller

Thomas Parnell

By Thomas M. Woodman

University of Reading

Twayne Publishers • Boston

Thomas Parnell

Thomas M. Woodman

Frontispiece reproduced from *The Poetical Works of Thomas Parnell,*
Aldine Edition (London: George Bell and Sons, 1894).

Book Production by Elizabeth Todesco
Book Design by Barbara Anderson

Printed on permanent/durable acid-free
paper and bound in the United States of
America.

**Library of Congress Cataloging in
Publication Data**

Woodman, Thomas M.
    Thomas Parnell.

    (Twayne's English authors series; TEAS 397)
    Bibliography: p. 130
    Includes index.
    1. Parnell, Thomas, 1679–1718
Criticism and interpretation.
I. Title.   II. Series.
PR3616.Z5W66   1985   821'.5   84–15676
ISBN 0–8057–6883–1

Contents

About the Author

Thomas M. Woodman, Lecturer in English at the University of Reading, England, received his B.A. at Jesus College, Oxford University, in 1968 and his M.Phil. in the Eighteenth Century from the same university two years later. In 1973 he received his Ph.D. from Yale University. He has taught at Oxford, Yale, St. David's College, Lampeter (University of Wales), and in his present position at Reading he lectures on Alexander Pope. Among his publications are an article on Pope and the topic of politeness in *Essays in Criticism* and an essay on the theological implications of science fiction in a book of collected essays.

Preface

Thomas Parnell won considerable fame as a poet in the eighteenth century. He was a friend of such men as Alexander Pope, Jonathan Swift, and Bishop Berkeley, and his work was praised in the highest terms by writers of the eminence of David Hume and the Warton brothers. Dr. Samuel Johnson's circle quoted and discussed him frequently, and Oliver Goldsmith used him as a weapon in his campaign against the literary tendencies represented in the later poetry of Thomas Gray. Even in the nineteenth century he was extravagantly praised. Edmund Gosse, for example, considered "The Hermit" "as forming the apex and *chef d'oeuvre* of Augustan poetry in England."

In this century Parnell has received little attention. There are a few articles, and general scholarly recognition of the historical importance of "A Night Piece on Death." There has never been a full critical edition, though one is now in preparation.

In this study I have set Parnell in the context of the various poetic traditions of his period. He is of particular interest in his development from a poet in the Protestant biblical sublime tradition to an elegant and classical occasional poet as presented by Pope in his selection from his friend's works. In tracing this development I survey not only the Christian poems that were not published until thirty-six years after Pope's selection but also material as yet unpublished. I have devoted my main attention, however, to the poems Pope selected for his *Poems on Several Occasions by Dr. Thomas Parnell* (1722). Pope's taste, in fact, seems to have been almost unerring. Most of the work he leaves out is not of the highest quality, though some of it is of real interest. The volume he edits presents Parnell as the epitome of an early eighteenth-century polite poet, the author of elegant society verse, classical in tone but with a touching emotionalism, pleasant nature description, and genuine Christian feeling.

In the poems from this short volume, itself only a small selection from the total work, Parnell reveals himself to be a poet of considerable charm and talent. The Christian sentiment and nature description of "The Hermit" and "A Night Piece on Death" in particular were of the greatest influence in the eighteenth century. Later they even led Parnell to be regarded as a "preromantic" poet in some quarters. The story of Parnell's reputation as a poet is itself an interesting one. As George Saintsbury says: "It is curious that, out of the small bulk of Parnell's poetical work, poetical criticism of the most various times and tastes has been able to pick quite different things to sustain his reputation." The study of this development is illuminating about the history of taste as well as about Parnell's work itself. Overall, it is surely clear that, despite what some critics have said, Parnell was no startling innovator but an interesting and representative man of letters of the period. He is worth study in this respect, but also because he produced a handful of poems whose influence was considerable, even if their significance was altered by their imitators. The charm and interest of these poems led critics to make extravagant claims for their originality at times when the critical stock at the period itself was low. Instead of seeing Parnell as the precursor of something new, however, we should allow his work to give us an expanded sense of the possibilities of poetry in his own period.

My interest in Parnell was first aroused by some eloquent comments on him by Donald Davie in *Purity of Diction in English Verse.* I was lucky enough to be able to discuss his work with Rachel Trickett and Roger Lonsdale during my M.Phil. in Oxford. At Yale I had the advice of Michael O'Loughlin. I wish to thank my friend Alan Munton for encouraging me to write to Twayne Publishers, and Professor Bertram Davis for his kind and helpful response. My colleague Ron Knowles has also given me the benefit of his knowledge of the period. Professor C. J. Rawson of Warwick University and F. P. Lock generously gave me the opportunity of reading Parnell's unpublished poems which they are preparing for their definitive edition. I would like to thank them for their friendliness and hospitality. Dave and Sue Cook were a great help with the typing. My parents and my wife Rosemary have always been very supportive during my work on Parnell and deserve the warmest thanks.

I wish to thank the editors of *Essays in Criticism* for their permission to reprint material from an article of mine on Parnell that first appeared there.

Thomas M. Woodman

University of Reading

Chronology

1718   Pays summer visit to England, and dies on the way home at Chester, aged thirty-nine.

1721   At end of the year Pope brings out *Poems on Several Occasions, by the late Dr. Parnell.*

1758   *The Posthumous Works of Dr. Thomas Parnell, containing poems Moral and Divine.*

Chapter One
Parnell's Life and Times

In a beautiful line Alexander Pope praises Thomas Parnell for being "with softest Manners, gentlest Arts, adorn'd."[1] Pope is clearly making a link here between his friend's well-known social gifts and his qualities as a poet. His fine "politeness" relates to what is etymologically the same word, the "polish" of his poetry. This, like Edmund Waller's correctness, is a quality we are unlikely to estimate as highly as eighteenth-century readers did. Yet it made Parnell a famous poet, and attempts to define the quality in terms of pure diction, elegance, simplicity, and a beautiful casualness occur time and time again in the chorus of praise of Parnell by Pope, Swift, David Hume, Goldsmith, Johnson, and the Warton brothers.[2]

The social and literary quality they called "politeness" seemed of very central importance in the early eighteenth century. James Miller wrote in 1738 that it was:

> The Coxcomb's Av'rice, Courtier's Claim,
> The Cit's Ambition, and the Soldier's Fame,[3]

and, asked what he considered the "Chief Qualification of a good Poet," Steele replied, "To be a very well-bred Man."[4] In the different influences in Thomas Parnell's social background we shall be able to see some of the factors that help to make his work the epitome of early eighteenth-century polite verse.

Social Background and Early Life

The basic outlines of Parnell's life are well established, and enough other references exist to form the conception of a personality.[5] He was the scion of a family long settled at Congleton in Cheshire, but with Irish connections. This was not an old-established gentry family. Its main line seems to have consisted of prosperous merchants. The poet's father was able, however, to leave his son what has been called "a considerable estate" in Ireland, as well as land in Cheshire.

Like the majority of the merchants and professional men, the elder Thomas Parnell was a supporter of Oliver Cromwell and he is said to have been a friend of the regicide, Thomas Bradshaw. It would be a mistake, though, to think that this meant that he ever left the Church of England. Before the Civil Wars Puritans saw themselves as members of a national Church which they wished to purify. During the Commonwealth period the national Church itself was largely Presbyterian in orientation. At the Restoration the poet's father, an alderman, refused to take the oath of office under Charles II and emigrated to Ireland, where other branches of the family had already settled. Yet he was always a low-church Anglican rather than a Dissenter, and the poet was baptized in the parish church of St. Catherine's, Dublin, on 14 September 1679.

Despite the divergences, there was considerable common ground between the more pious gentry, merchants and professional men, whether they were from dissenting, low-church or even high-church Anglican backgrounds. They were likely to disapprove both of the excesses of the Restoration court and of the more enthusiastic elements among the sectarians after the Civil Wars. Earnest in their Christianity, they shared an interest in a biblically inspired moral literature, and admired, for example, the biblical poetry of Abraham Cowley. Jeremy Collier's attack on the Restoration theater is indistinguishable from what might be considered Puritan influences, yet he was in fact a high-church non-juror, one of those who refused to take the oath of allegiance to William of Orange. Among Thomas Parnell's own early undergraduate poems is a eulogy of Collier.[6]

For several centuries the educational interests and opportunities of the prosperous classes had been improving. In 1692 Parnell was admitted at the early age of thirteen to Trinity College, Dublin, where he took the degrees of B.A. in 1697 and M.A. in 1700. In the latter year he was ordained deacon by the distinguished Dr. William King, then Bishop of Derry, who was one of his guardians. On 25 April 1701 King wrote to Parnell's tutor, Mr. Lloyd, urging him to encourage Parnell in the serious and pious resolutions that he appeared to have embraced.[7] University education at this time was, of course, heavily classical in orientation, and it provided, along with the earnest biblical emphasis, the other main background influence on Parnell's work.

A period of indecision about ordination to the priesthood followed and King wrote in 1702 that Parnell had been melancholy.[8] In

1704, however, the ordination went ahead, and he was installed the same year as minor canon of St. Patrick's Cathedral, Dublin. It has been suggested that his friendship with Jonathan Swift, so important a factor in his life, dates from this time when Swift held the prebend of Dunlavin in the same cathedral. In 1706 King was able to help his protégé become Archdeacon of Clogher, with the parish of Clontilibret attached. Next month King, now Archbishop, sent Parnell a letter of advice on his pastoral duties. A tone of religious solemnity pervades the whole:

. . . there is too often an airiness and humour of pleasantry in young men that makes them decline the appearance of great concern in religious matters, and hide the true sense they have of it. There is nothing more shocking to country people (especially to those amongst whom you live) than this gaiety and *à la mode* of negligence as to divine matters, and therefore you must guard yourself against it with the utmost care, and when you have done all you can you will find that many words and actions that you by custom use innocently will be uneasy to them, and therefore you must take care to use all means to persuade them that you are in earnest, that you teach them religion, not because it is your profession, or because you are to make advantages by it, but because it is truly the sense of your heart; and because it is so, it will on all occasions season your conversation and actions. This is a thing so material that till you put them out of all doubt about it your preaching will have little influence on them . . . ; you are to mind diligently the canons and rubrics of our Church, your ordination promises, and above all the commands of God in the Holy Scripture, of which relating to your office, and the obligation to perform it, I would have you make a collection and endeavour to conform your practice to them.[9]

The archbishop also warns Parnell against intemperance and un-chastity, for which marriage is, he says, the surest remedy. The whole letter is an impressive witness to the earnestness sometimes found in high places in early eighteenth-century Anglicanism.

Perhaps Parnell heeded his mentor's advice about chastity, for his new appointment was soon followed, though we have no exact dates, by his marriage to Anne Minchin of Tipperary, whom tradition holds to have been a beauty. Parnell's "When thy beauty appears" is said to refer to his wife, and another song uses her nickname Nancy. Two sons and one daughter were born of the marriage, but both sons predeceased their father. Parnell's marriage seems to have been a happy one, and several different sources emphasize his terrible grief on her death in 1711. Swift states that "I believe the poor lad is much afflicted; they appeared to live perfectly well together," and nearly a year later, "It seems he has been ill for grief of his Wives death." He also tells a rather sad story about the first occasion when he and the poet dined at Lord Bolingbroke's: "Ldy Bolingbr– came down to us at dinner and Parnell stared at her as if she were a Goddess. I thought she was like Parnell's wife; and he thought so too."[10] Such comments have been enough for critics to claim that both *Spectator* no. 501 on the subject of grief and the "Night Piece" are about Parnell's personal experience of bereavement.

The London Literary World and the Scriblerus Club

Parnell's visits to London had begun before the death of his wife. He was reacquainted with Swift on one of the earlier visits or during the longer period of travel in England after her death. Directly, or through the friendship of Swift, he made contact with the Whig writers Joseph Addison and Richard Steele, from whom Swift was not yet estranged. These influential essayists saw their role as that of improving the manners and morals of the gentry and the more prosperous of the merchants and urban professional men. Interest both in the arts and in matters of politeness and fashion had been growing for some time. The improvement in education before the Restoration, the increased prosperity after it, the development of communications, the French influence at the court, the growth of London and the London season, and the new journalism all contributed.

Addison and Steele self-consciously combined moral seriousness with polite stylishness. Their Christian gentleman went to heaven "with a very good Mien," and it was their ambition to see the day "when it shall be as much the Fashion among men of Politeness to admire a Rapture of St. Paul, as any fine expression in Virgil or Horace: and to see a well dressed young man produce an Evangelist out of his pocket and be no more out of countenance than if it were a Classick printed by Elzevir."[11] Their influence on Parnell was of the greatest significance in modifying some of the more heavy-handed and didactic quality in his work. On 18 August and 4 October 1711 he contributed allegorical papers to the *Spectator*, the first of his works to appear in print. Then in 1713 several of his poems appeared in Steele's *Poetical Miscellanies*.

Perhaps through attachment to the interests of the Church, like Swift, perhaps through Swift's own influence, or perhaps even through a touch of careerism, Parnell began to side with the Tories, who were in office from 1711. The rise of party politics had meant that for some time now the old system of court patronage was supplemented by a newer form of political patronage. In the past poets had sometimes received court sinecures. Now they were taken up as men of talent, useful for other services than poetry, as pamphleteers or even as diplomats like Addison and Matthew Prior. A contemporary writer commented that "we see men of polite parts snatch'd up from Pen-Ink Labours to the greatest Employment in the Government, made Parliament-men, Commissioners, Secretaries of State—etc."[12]

Parnell's friendship with Swift drew him rapidly into this kind of world. Swift recognized in him a man of talent and tried to obtain for him a post with the Commission that was to accept the surrender of Dunkirk, but the plan fell through. The government was headed by Robert Harley, Earl of Oxford. The other main influence in it was Harley's rival, Henry St. John, Viscount Bolingbroke. In December 1712 Swift showed Lord Bolingbroke Parnell's *Essay on the Different Styles of Poetry*. He had suggested that Parnell insert some compliments to the politician, and Bolingbroke was "extremely pleased with it, and read some parts of it to-day to Ld Treasurer [Oxford], who liked it as much; and indeed he outdoes all our Poets here a Barr's Length." Later that month Swift "carried Parnell to dine at Ld Bolingbroke's and he behaved himself very well, and Ld Bolingbroke is mightily pleased with him." On December 31 Bolingbroke showed Parnell all the parts of the poem he disliked, and Parnell was to correct it before publication. With typical dilatoriness and much to Swift's annoyance he had still not carried out the corrections by 17 January of the next year. On 31 January Swift introduced Oxford to Parnell. The story is told that when Lord Oxford was informed that Parnell was among the crowd in the outer room, he went at Swift's persuasion, "with his treasurer's staff in his hand to enquire for him." Swift was proud that it was done that way round: "I value myself on making the Ministry desire to be acquainted with Parnell, and not Parnell with the Ministry."[13]

When the *Essay on the Different Styles of Poetry* was finally published
in March 1713, Swift said that it was "mightily esteemed, but
Poetry sells ill." George Berkeley, later the bishop and famous
philosopher, who knew Parnell personally, calls it a "very fine"
poem in a letter to Sir John Perceval.[14] In the same year Parnell
contributed two *Guardian* essays and wrote a poem to welcome the
Tory Peace of Utrecht.

It was during this period that, as Pope wrote to John Gay on 23
October 1713, Parnell entered "heartily" into the design to publish
a monthly periodical to be called *The Works of the Unlearned*.[15] This
was the origin of the Scriblerus Club, of which Parnell, Pope, Swift,
Gay, John Arbuthnot, and Harley, Lord Oxford, were members.
Undeniably the Scriblerus Club made up a group of the finest writers
and greatest wits in England. For a time Swift at least was politically
influential, and all of them mixed almost as equals with aristocratic
politicians at the very height of power. Lord Oxford in particular
spent many evenings with the group, relaxed from the cares of state,
in response to pleasant verse invitations like the following from
Parnell:

> For Frolick Mirth give oer affairs of State,
> To night be happy, be to morrow great.[16]

Nostalgically he wrote to Pope three years after Parnell's death, "I
look back indeed to those evenings I have usefully and pleasantly
spent with Mr. Pope, Dr. Parnell, Dean Swift, the Doctor Arbuthnot etc."[17]

Accounts of this time in letters and journals give a pleasant
impression of genuine friendships, high spirits, and intellectual
vivacity. One example shows Parnell's quick intelligence and gift
for teasing. While Pope was reading the unfinished *Rape of the Lock,*
Parnell managed to commit the description of Belinda's dressing
table to memory. During the night he turned it into Latin verse
and insisted the next day that Pope had stolen part of the description
from an old manuscript. On another occasion the Scriblerians decided to walk out into the country to the home of Lord Bathurst
for dinner and to stay the night. Swift, who walked fast, hurried
on ahead. Afraid that he would claim the best bed, Parnell rode on
horseback in order to arrive first and persuaded the host to send out
a servant to warn Swift that there was smallpox in the house. While

the others dined, Swift was given a cold supper and told he must sleep in the summer-house, but eventually his friends relented and allowed him to join the company. [18]

It is no wonder that this time made an indelible impression on all these men and influenced widely divergent literary enterprises like *The Beggar's Opera, Gulliver's Travels,* and *The Dunciad.* All these works retain the mark of such intimacy and intellectual daring in relaxed circumstances. Parnell's intellectual contacts with this group combined with the influence of Addison and Steele to produce his remarkable development from a biblical "sublime" and didactic poet to a poet of courtly elegance and wit in the polite tradition. Pope and the other poets of the group preserved many of the older courtly attitudes to poetry. They sought wit and a stylish ease of manner, and, despite their deep moral seriousness, they were also attracted by an irreverent skepticism more characteristic of Restoration circles. They attacked all forms of what they regarded as pedantry, and they continued court traditions in particular in their dislike of a heavy-handed didactic tone and in their Restoration suspicion of religious enthusiasm.

Parnell's exact contribution to the club's projects cannot now be clearly determined. Charles Kerby-Miller, the editor of *The Memoirs of Martinus Scriblerus,* sees no reason to doubt Pope's statement that he, Arbuthnot, and Parnell wrote in conjunction the "Essay concerning the Origin of the Sciences," a mock-learned piece to prove that modern man derived the arts and sciences from the ancient pygmies. [19] Later, however, Swift remarked of the Scriblerus undertaking, "Parnell has some ideas of it, but is idle," and Pope was to comment in a letter to Arbuthnot that Parnell had greatly neglected the memory of Scriblerus. [20]

During some of this period Parnell also stayed with Pope at Binfield and spent considerable time helping him with the Homeric translations, as an amusing letter by Pope from 1714 makes plain:

. . . The minute I lost you, Eustathius with nine hundred pages, and nine thousand Contractions of the Greek Character, Arose to my View— Spondamus with all his Auxiliaries, in Number a thousand pages (Value three shillings) and Dacier's three Volumes, Barnes's two, Valterie's three, Cuperus half in Greek, Leo Allatius three parts in Greek, Scaliger, Macrobius, and (worse than 'em all) Aulus Gellius: all these Rushd upon my Soul at once and whelm'd me under a fit of the Head Ach. . . . Dear

Sir, not only as you are a friend and as you are a Good natur'd man, but as you are Christian and a Divine, come back speedily and prevent the Encrease of my Sins: For at the Rate I have begun to rave, I shall not only Damn all the Poets and Commentators who have gone before me, but be damned myself by all who come after me—

Beneath the ironic self-depreciation of the letter Pope meant what he said. Parnell was a good scholar and his help with Pope's inadequacies was priceless: "you are Generous Author, I a Hackney Scribler, you are a Grecian and bred at a University; I a poor Englishman of my own Educating . . ."[21] Such assistance was crowned by Parnell's lengthy "Essay on the Life, Writings and Learning of Homer" prefixed to Pope's *Iliad*. Of his friend, Pope wrote in the Preface that his "good-nature (to give it a high panegyric) is no less extensive than his learning," and in the last volume of the translation, published when Parnell was already dead:

The whole Essay upon Homer was written upon such Memoirs as I had collected, by the late Dr. Parnell, Archdeacon of Clogher in Ireland. How very much that Gentleman's Friendship prevailed over his Genius in detaining a Writer of his Spirit in the drudgery of removing the Rubbish of past Pedants, will soon appear to the World, when they shall see those beautiful Pieces of Poetry, the Publication of which he left to my charge, almost with his dying breath.[22]

With the fall of the Oxford ministry and the death of Queen Anne everything changed. Bolingbroke wrote in memorable words, "The Earl of Oxford was removed on Tuesday, the Queen died on Sunday. What a world is this, and how does fortune banter us."[23] The Tory group could hope for no favor from the Hanoverians, and the friends separated. Late in 1714 Parnell himself returned to Ireland. There can be no doubt that he was a disappointed man. There are stories that he had become by this time a well-known preacher in the city and around Southwark. His literary talents and his friendships with the great must have given him hopes of preferment. Earlier in 1714 he had been optimistic about receiving from Oxford the post of chaplain in an embassy to Hanover. The death of the Queen and the change of government finally dashed his hopes. His mind was certainly dominated by the glamour of the London literary world and, allowing for humorous hyperbole, his lines to Pope on the relative dullness of Ireland are heartfelt:

> For Fortune plac'd me in unfertile ground;
> Far from the joys that with my soul agree,
> From wit, from learning—far, O far from thee.[24]

Owen Ruffhead, indeed, attributes Parnell's problems with alcohol to this disappointment.[25] In September 1714 Parnell wrote to Arbuthnot in terms that pleasantly recalled the whole Scriblerian enterprise, and yet in such a way that the flippancy does not conceal the sadness: "It is a pleasure to us to recollect the Satisfaction we enjoyed in your company, when we used to meet the Dean and Gay with you; and Greatness itself condescended to look in at the Door to us. Then it was that the immortal Scriblerus Smild upon our endeavours, who now hangs his head in an obscure corner, pining for his friends that are Scattering over the face of the earth. Yet art thou still, O Scriblerus, as deserving of our Lucubrations."[26]

On 31 May 1716 Archbishop King presented Parnell with the vicarage of Finglass. Several letters from Pope to Parnell during this period after his return to Ireland refer to Parnell's poem *The Battle of the Frogs and Mice* with *The Remarks and Life of Zoilus*. The translation was most probably prepared in late 1714 or before the late spring of 1715, but it was not published until May 1717. The poem, the mock-learned notes, and the *Life* of the bad critic were the first Scriblerian works to be published. They also helped Pope in the controversy about his translation of Homer, and they apparently delighted him. A fine mark of Parnell's personal generosity is that the copy money was given to the impoverished John Gay.

In the summer of 1718 Parnell was once more in London. In nostalgic mood Pope, Parnell, and Gay sent to Lord Oxford, who had been imprisoned in the Tower for alleged Jacobite offenses, some doggerel verses from:

> One that should be a saint [Parnell]
> And one that's a sinner [Gay]
> And one that pays reckning [Pope]
> but ne'r eats a dinner.[27]

The reunion was brief. Parnell left for Ireland in October, but was taken ill on his way at Chester, and died suddenly there on 24 October at the age of thirty-nine. He was buried in the churchyard

of Holy Trinity Church in that city. Pope wrote to the painter Jervas
in December enquiring about a monument, but he said at the same
time that the volume of Parnell's poems he would bring out would
be the best monument he could erect.[28]

At the end of 1721, prefaced by a beautiful poem to Lord Oxford
in the poet's memory, the volume appeared. It is clear both from
Pope's own remarks and from what later appeared elsewhere that
Pope had published only a fraction of what his friend had written.

The Personality and the Poetry

One thing that is immediately obvious about Parnell's personality
is that he was the possessor of great social charm. This comes out
in the Scriblerus Club anecdotes and in other details of his life. As
Goldsmith says, "How much his company was desired, appears from
the extensiveness of his conversations and the number of his friends."[29]
His gifts as a conversationalist, his good nature, the pleasure of his
companionship are testified to everywhere. Pope's letters breathe
genuine affection, complaining that he fears "one of the best naturd
men alive neglects me." He goes on to say: "All this is as true as
that we are sincerely Lovers of you, and Deplorers of your absence;
and that we form no wish more zealously than that which brings
you over to us. . . . We have lately had some distant hopes of the
Dean's design to revisit England. Will you not accompany him? or
is England to lose everything that has any charm for us? and must
we pray for Banishment or a Benediction?" Elsewhere he testifies
delightedly to Parnell's effect on others after the latter's first stay
at Binfield to help with Homer: ". . . you have wrought Several
Miracles upon our Family; you have made old people fond of a
Young and gay Person and Inveterate Papists of a Clergyman of the
Church of England—even Nurse herself is in danger of being in
Love in her old Age and (for all I know) would even marry Dennis
for your Sake because he is your man and loves his Master."[30]

There is also ample evidence for a darker side to the picture.
Parnell was obviously, for example, of unstable physical health.
Archbishop King wrote and advised him not to accept a demanding
Dublin parish because of this constitutional weakness and sickness.[31]
But the instability was more than purely physical. There is irre-
futable evidence of an almost manic-depressive temperament. Swift
referred to his friend's neurosis: "the poor lad is almost always out

of order with his head," and Pope wrote to Parnell, "I have been once a witness of some, (I hope all) of your splenetic hours."[32] P. S. Schoedinger has interestingly interpreted Swift's comment to mean that Parnell, like Swift, had Menière's disease of the inner ear. This would cause dizziness, too, and perhaps explain the rumors of drunkenness. These latter stories, however, whether explained uncharitably by thwarted ambition or charitably as a reaction to bereavement, are surely too numerous to be confuted, and they are found as early as Thomas Hearne.[33]

The question of Parnell's drunkenness fascinated James Boswell and Samuel Johnson for their own different reasons, and the whole issue became important to the development of realistic biography. Boswell at one stage suggested that the question was "whether a man's vices should be mentioned," for if people knew that Addison and Parnell drank too freely they would "probably more easily indulge in drinking from knowing this." Johnson turned this argument on its head: "When I [Boswell] objected to the danger of telling that Parnell drank to excess, he said that it would produce an instructive caution to avoid drinking when it was seen that even the learning and genius of Parnell could be debased by it." Boswell was convinced by this argument and took up the example himself in the *Life of Johnson,* his own masterpiece of realistic biography, itself strongly influenced by Johnson's theories: "Nor can I apprehend that more harm can ensue from the knowledge of the irregularity of Johnson, guarded as I have stated it, than from knowing that Addison and Parnell were intemperate in their use of wine, which he himself in his 'Lives' of those celebrated writers and pious men, has not foreborne to record."[34]

Parnell's life is relevant to his poetry in certain obvious ways. We find no reason, for example, to doubt the sincerity of his religious convictions, for as Johnson points out, a man of Archbishop King's probity would hardly have given preferment to Parnell otherwise. (This would also incidentally suggest that the drinking could not have been as flagrant as some have implied.) The genuine classical learning is also of the highest relevance to the poems. But Parnell's most characteristic poetry combines classicism and a religious impulse with an interest in sentiment and what has even been considered emotionalism. Here we are on shakier ground. To jump from these aspects of his temperament to his poetry would be foolish. The critics who do so are the exponents of Parnell as a so-called "preromantic" poet. They exaggerate such elements in his work or even invoke the romantic myth of the poet. The emotionalism of Parnell's better poetry is, however, beautifully restrained, and subsumed by his artistic purposes.

Whatever the dangers of speculating in other ways about the relationship between Parnell's poetry and his biography, this was obviously a period in which there was the closest possible connection between social life and poetry. The link Pope makes in the line quoted at the beginning of the chapter between his friend's social graces and the marvelous polish and social assurance of his art was surely justified.

Chapter Two
The Posthumous Poems of Dr. Thomas Parnell (1758)

"Poems Divine and Moral"

Late in 1716 Parnell sent Pope a collection of his poetic manuscripts. He intended that Pope, with his professional expertise and literary contacts, should look them over, correct them where necessary, and prepare them for the press. Involved with his mammoth task of translating Homer, Pope delayed his work on Parnell's poems and only completed it after his friend's death. The beautifully presented *Poems on Several Occasions* was published at the end of 1721. Pope said clearly that he had omitted many poems, for "What he gave me to publish was but a small part of what he left behind him; but it was the best, and I will not make it worse by enlarging it." He later burnt copies of the poems he did not include, and said to Spence that they would not add anything to the Dean's character.[1]

Throughout almost the whole of the rest of the century other poems of Parnell's were published, starting with four included in a volume printed in Dublin in 1726. The controversial *Posthumous Poems of Dr. Thomas Parnell* was published in 1758. P. S. Schoedinger prints in his Yale Ph. D. thesis other previously unpublished poems written while Parnell was an undergraduate.[2] Professor Rawson of Warwick University also has some seventy additional unpublished poems of Parnell's in preparation for his definitive edition with F. P. Lock.

The poems not included in Pope's edition can be categorized as secular or religious. The first category includes the interesting *Essay on the Different Styles of Poetry*, some classical and occasional pieces and a handful of unpublished satires and elegies. The religious category, the subject of this chapter, consists of lengthy biblical paraphrases or short hymns.

13

Traditions of Biblical Poetry

Parnell's undergraduate poems printed by P. S. Schoedinger are
of no poetic merit, but their subjects show his earnest piety. There
are four versified psalms, a "Meditation before the Sacrament" (which
is surely the sign of specifically Anglican influence), and a poem
called "The Penitent Sinner." There is also a eulogy of Jeremy
Collier, famous for his diatribe on the Restoration theater, which
shows that Parnell associated himself at this time with the pious
reformers of manners. Another poem, "Of Content," is an early
version of the theme of the later "Hymn to Contentment."

The poems in the 1758 volume reveal somewhat more facility
than these earliest attempts and more self-consciousness. They are
a natural continuation of the traditions behind these earliest poems.
Yet they are so different from the poems Pope selected that their
authenticity has been questioned. The *Critical Review,* for example,
announced with confidence when they first appeared, that: "These
poems are spurious. We cannot easily persuade ourselves that so
elegant, pure, and spirited a Writer could ever fall so far beneath
himself as to let such flat and insipid stuff as this whole volume is
drop from his pen. . . . Nothing sure can be more unlike Dr.
Parnell. . . . They seem rather to resemble the wild and non-
sensical hymns of a mad Moravian, than the remains of so excellent
a writer as the late Dr. Parnell." Dr. Johnson himself said of these
poems "I know not whence they come, nor have ever enquired
whither they are going: they stand upon the faith of the compilers."[3]

It can scarcely be denied that the volume is of inferior quality
overall. Its authenticity is nevertheless now beyond doubt. Professor
Rawson has established that a manuscript notebook of the *Posthumous
Poems* in the British Museum is probably in Parnell's handwriting.
He has also established that the "Benjamin Everard" referred to in
the Preface to the published volume was a close associate of the
poet.[4] Study of these poems is indeed essential to an understanding
of the poet's whole development.

Parnell's family background was in the Protestant commercial
classes, as we have seen, though the family was assimilated to the
low-church wing of the Church of England rather than nonconfor-
mism. The elder Thomas Parnell was prosperous enough to buy an
estate in Ireland and to provide a university education for his son.
This whole social grouping often preserved traditions of piety and

moral seriousness. In literature its more educated members admired an earnest biblical poetry.

Ever since the Reformation the virtues of the Bible as the inspiration for poetry had been particularly emphasized and traditions of biblical epic, paraphrase, and hymns had developed. In France there was a flourishing movement of this kind, and the appearance of the King James authorized version encouraged it in England too. Du Bartas's poem to the muse of Christian poetry, Urania, was translated into English by Sylvester and became seminal.[5] This Christian muse appears to the poet like an angelic visitant and converts his heart away from the idolatry of secular verse to zealous religious poetry. There were important reworkings of the idea in George Herbert and many other poets. With Cowley we find the same idea combined with an attempt at biblical epic in the French mode in the *Davideis* and a manifesto on behalf of biblical poetry.

As the case of Cowley would indicate, there was no absolute divorce between the biblical and the courtly-classical traditions. The *Davideis* conveys the biblical story in a classical tone and style. Matthew Prior's prime allegiances lay with the courtly traditions of wit, yet he produced his own biblical epic, *Solomon,* and Pope wrote "Messiah." The dissenting poet Isaac Watts on the other hand paid a noble tribute to the beneficent influence of Horace.[6] Yet the two traditions were felt as distinct in tone and outlook, and most poets of the time can be seen as belonging primarily to one or the other.

Cowley also popularized the Pindaric ode, a genre in which wildness, high flights, and the sublime were expected, and his own attempts linked this with religious poetry. As Longinus, the late classical exponent of the sublime, grew popular, the link became closer. He had instanced "Let there be light" from Genesis as a prime example of the sublime.[7] Mystical flight itself became a central motif with Cowley's "The Ecstasie," an imitation of several of the Polish Jesuit Cassimire Sarbiewski's neo-Latin poems. Trance, ascent to the skies, flight through the heavens are the traditional imagery of mystical experience. The biblical sources are Elijah's ascent and St. Paul's rapture into the seventh heaven. The imagery was elaborated in Neoplatonic mysticism, and popularized, for example, in Boethius's *Consolation.* In the Middle Ages it became associated with an elaborate system of purification from earthly attachments, leading ultimately to the beatific vision, whether in this life or after death. Protestant mysticism was obviously different from Catholic, but the Anglican writers were eclectic and even the Dissenters often retained much of the older imagery. Certainly an erotic mystical imagery is found in the Dissenters Watts and Mrs. Rowe as well as the imagery of trance, ascension, and flying. The tradition of biblical poetry and legitimate "enthusiasm" was elaborated, following Cowley, by John Dennis, Sir Richard Blackmore, and Isaac Watts. It attained to the status of a movement, a reaction against Restoration excesses linked with the idea of the reformation of manners in the period. The mystical imagery was thus itself blended with the classical motif of the poet carried on the wings of Pegasus to stress the enthusiasm and sublime flights of the true, biblically oriented poet. A further link was sometimes also made with the idea of Newtonian exploration of the universe, so that the flight through the heavens becomes as much an astronomical tour as a mystical ascent or sublime aspiration.[8] In general it must certainly be said that the genuine mystical note became rarer, replaced by a didactic quality and an unconvincing attempt at the sublime.

The 1758 Volume

In "Piety, or The Vision," the first poem in the 1758 volume, Parnell gives a direct reworking of Du Bartas's "Urania" as translated by Sylvester. The angel of piety appears to Parnell, purifies his lips, like Isaiah's, with burning coal and tells him to forego secular poetry and make his "muse thy zeal." Parnell is then swept up into a vision of Christ and Heaven. Yet a touch of skepticism and self-doubt remains:

> But still I fear, unwarm'd with holy flames
> I take for truth the Flatteries of a dream.
>
> (A, 114)

This is not only the conventional modesty expected from the young poet but also a reflection of some of the period's suspicion of "enthusiasm," a suspicion that coexisted with the cult of inspiration.[9]

One important element in the tradition of biblical poetry was the defense of poetry itself because of its presence in the sacred writings. This led to a great cult of figures like David. Sir Philip Sidney explained that "The chiefe poets both in antiquitie and excellencie were they that did imitate the inconceivable excellencies of GOD.

Such were David in his psalmes, Solomon in his songs, in his Ecclesiastes and Proverbs, Moses and Deborah in their Hymnes."[10] This underlies Parnell's choice of the stories in the lengthy biblical paraphrases that come under the general heading of "The Gift of Poetry." Parnell begins the series with another angelic visitant, the "Gift of Poetry" herself. He portrays himself looking through the sacred pages of the Bible and coming first to the "first-remembered song," that of Moses.

Biblical paraphrase was very popular in England throughout the whole period from the early sixteenth century to the middle of the eighteenth. It was practiced by poets who might surprise us, like Edmund Waller, and was part of the stock-in-trade of a typical early eighteenth-century poet like William Broome. As the example of Pope's "Messiah" would suggest, paraphrase does not mean dogged literalism. The relevant definition in Johnson's *Dictionary* (1755) is "to translate loosely." Thus the biblical paraphrase may be linked with the aspiration to poetic sublimity, and can be almost an original poem with scriptural imagery, style, and subject; or it can be a reasonably close reworking of specific biblical passages. On the whole Parnell's work is the latter. It seems safe to assume that these are what have been called his "apprentice" poems, the exercises of the young poet. Nevertheless, Parnell rearranges the narrative of the life of Moses to suit his own purposes and highlight certain aspects. Furthermore, at various points he speaks in his own person, using the biblical text as the jumping-off ground for a meditation of his own, as, for example, in a melodramatic reflection on death, which makes an interesting comparison with a "Night Piece":

> See ghastly Death, where deserts all around,
> Spread forth the barren undelightful ground;
> There stalks the silent melancholy shade,
> His naked bones reclining on a spade;
> And thrice the earth with solemn sadness heaves,
> And thrice earth opens in the form of graves,
> His gates of darkness gape, to take him in;
> And where he soon would sink, he's pushed by Sin.
>   (C, 374)

Similarly at the end of "Hannah" Parnell breaks out into a hymn of his own:

> Burst forth, my temper, in a godly flame,
> For all his blessings laud his holy name,
>   (C, 381)

and in "David" into a prophetic vision of Christ. He directly states
in "Deborah" what his aim in such passages is:

> Touch'd with a sacred rage and heavenly flame,
> I strive to sing thine universal aim.
> To quit the subject and in days sublime,
> The morals fit for any point of time.
>   (C, 379)

Most poets of the time were unable to resist an artificial heightening of style in their search for sublimity, though the noble simplicity of the biblical text was recognized. Parnell's version of "The
Lord is my Shepherd" is on the whole simple, despite the slightly
baroque line on death:

> The Lord's my shepherd, bountiful and good,
> I cannot want, since he provides me food;
> Me for his sheep along the verdant meads,
> Me, all too mean, his tender mercy leads,
> To taste the springs of life, and take repose,
> Wherever living pasture sweetly grows.
> And as I cannot want, I need not fear,
> For still the presence of my shepherd's near,
> Through darksome vales where beasts of prey resort,
> Where Death appears with all his dreadful Court,
> His rod and hook direct me where I stray,
> He calls to fold and they direct my way.
>   (C, 382–83)

Here the danger is rather one of an artless simplicity, verging on
naiveté.

In his own attempts at heightening Parnell is led into many
unfortunate habits of style. The worst is his uninspired use of anaphora or rhetorical repetition. Time and time again he uses the device
mechanically in an attempt at ornamentation of a pedestrian statement, otherwise expressed in a diction that is if anything too simple:

> My God, from whom proceed the gifts divine,
> My God, I think I feel the gift is thine,
>
> (C, 371)

> Oh, wake, my Fancy, for the glorious Theme,
> Oh, wake, my Fancy, with the sense of praise,
> Oh, wake with warblings of triumphant days.
>
> (C, 377)

Repetitions are one of the rhetorical devices discussed in Parnell's *Essay on the Different Styles of Poetry.* He also refers there to rhetorical questions, exclamations, apostrophes, and personifications, "the new creations of the muse." In these biblical paraphrases personifications are overelaborate, pictorial, and pseudo-Spenserian in comparison with the economic use in the poems Pope chose. The following personification of Despair is a clear example:

> See, where from Hell she breaks the crumbling ground,
> Her hairs stand upright, and they stare around;
> Her horrid front deep-trenching wrinkles trace,
> Lean sharpening looks deform her livid face;
> Bent lie the brows, and at the bend below,
> With fire and blood two wandering eye-balls glow.
> Fill'd are her arms with numerous aids to kill.
>
> (C, 397)

In Cowley's Pindaric odes an occasional self-consciousness about his attempts at the sublime reveals itself, a version of the old rhetorical device of "occupatio," the recognition of the unworthiness of verse and its inability to describe the indescribable. One example is the line from "The Resurrection": "Stop, stop, my muse, allay thy vig'rous heat."[11] Parnell's self-consciousness, his feeling of the difficulty of sustaining such elevated flights, is obviously greater than Cowley's. He is inclined to appeal to or apostrophize his "fancy" in an unfortunate way: "Now Fancy flag not as that subject ends" (C, 372), or "Begin my lines" (A, 193). Broadly speaking, his style is not adequate to sustain the visionary Pindaric flights to which he aspires. He makes himself look somewhat absurd by presenting himself in dialogue with angels and allegorical personages. He is inclined to describe the heavenly realms in an inflated baroque tone with the diction becoming bloated with ill-digested Miltonic words like *azure, ethereal,* and *lambent.* He is too ready, both in these biblical paraphrases and in the other religious poems, to take up the image of his being transported through the air in mystical ardor and Pindaric enthusiasm. This had by now become a cliché, as we have seen: it can be found in Cassimire, Cowley, Sir Richard Blackmore, Lady Mary Chudleigh, John Dennis, John Norris, Samuel Say, John Hughes, and Isaac Watts. [12]

In "Ecstacy" the "flight" is as follows:

> But whither, whither now? What powerful fire
> With this bless'd influence equals my desire?
> I rise (or Love, the kind deluder reigns
> And acts in fancy such enchanted scenes),
> Earth lessening flies, the parting skies retreat,
> The fleacy clouds my waning feathers beat,
> And now the sun and now the stars are gone.
>
> (A, 209–10)

The fall into appalling bathos is also, however, only too readily apparent:

> But where's my rapture, where my wondrous heat,
> What interuption makes my bliss retreat?
> This world's got in, the thoughts of t'others crost,
> And the gay picture's in my fancy lost.
>
> (A, 212)

At certain places in the biblical paraphrases Parnell writes with a passionate personal intensity and uses the traditional imagery of Christian erotic mysticism, as found, for example, in St. John of the Cross. At the end of "David" he writes:

> Then in my soul a mystic altar near,
> And such a sacrifice I'll offer there,
> There shall it stand, in vows of virtue bound,
> There falling tears shall wash it all around;
> And sharp remorse, yet sharper edg'd by woe,
> Deserv'd and fear'd, inflict the bleeding blow;
> There shall my thoughts to holy breathings fly,
> Instead of incense to perfume the sky,
> And there my willing heart aspires above
> A victim panting in the flames of love.
>
> (C, 390)

The last line in particular has an almost Counter-Reformation tone. Yet there was an overlap between Protestant and Catholic mysticism. The Song of Songs was itself the primary text for this quasi-erotic mysticism, taken up by Puritan and Anglican writers as well as by Catholics. In "Solomon" Parnell makes clear in the traditional fashion that the erotic song is an allegory of Christ's love for His Church. Parnell could have come in contact with religious poetry in this tradition in the works of Edward Benlowes, Henry Vaughan, and John Norris among others. The poems of the Baptist Thomas Harrison, a near-contemporary, show how widespread it was. In Harrison's work too is found all the imagery of wings and flights, of light and heat, of flaming love, as well as of sudden returns to earth:

> But suddenly the pleasing vision fled,
> Awak'd I lay lamenting on my Bed
> That still I must remain
> Without Relief amidst perplexing cares,
> Encompassed by num'rous hidden snares,
> And drag a heavy chain. [13]

It was in hymns and religious lyrics in particular that a special biblical simplicity was sought, as well as in some cases the intensity of personal religious feeling and mystical ardor. A hymn is usually characterized by a regular quatrain structure and a chastity of diction. It is rarely complicated by any kind of literary sophistication. Though the Church of England made no use of congregational hymns at this time, the general stylistic aim was certainly that expressed by Isaac Watts in the preface to his *Hymns and Spiritual Songs* (1707): "The metaphors are generally sunk to the level of vulgar capacities. I have aimed at ease of Numbers and Smoothness of Sound, and endeavour'd to make the sense plain and obvious." [14]

Parnell's three poems entitled "Hymns" retain this simplicity of tone. They may have had some connection with the idea of matins and evensong, though the inclusion of a hymn for noon would argue against this. These hymns in which nature and the sun are neatly used as analogues for spiritual truth have been praised recently. [15] In their extreme, often monosyllabic simplicity and their rather singsong octosyllabic meters they nevertheless achieve an unfortunately naive effect:

> Whate'er we think, whate'er we do,
> His glory still be kept in view.
> O Giver of eternal bliss!
> Heavenly Father! grant me this
> Grant it all as well as me,
> All whose hearts are fix'd on thee,
> Who revere thy Son above,
> Who thy sacred Spirit love.
> ("Hymn for Morning," A, 187)

Much the same is true of the other short religious lyrics. The
simplicity of tone is deliberate, but too extreme:

> Guide me, then, for here I burn
> To make my Saviour some return.
> I'll rise (if that will please him still,
> And sure I've heard him own it will),
> I'll trace his steps and bear my cross,
> Despising every grief and loss,
> Since he, despising pain and shame,
> First took up his and did the same.
> (A, 196)

The emotional directness is no doubt genuine enough, but it is
artless in a pejorative sense.

"The Happy Man" is similar in theme to a "Hymn to Contentment" and the "Allegory on Man." Parnell says of the soul:

> Its knowing real interest lies
> On the bright side of yonder skies,
> Where having made a title fair,
> It mounts, and leaves the world to Care;
> While he that seeks for pleasing days,
> In earthly joys and evil ways,
> Is but the fool of Toil or Fame
> (Though happy be the specious name),
> And made by wealth, which makes him great,
> A more conspicuous wretch of state.
> (A, 198–99)

The last line is quite powerful, but on the whole we are likely to
think how much better all this is expressed in the "Hymn to Con-

tentment" or in the obliquer fable of the "Allegory on Man," where "leaves the world to Care" becomes a vivid personification. "The Way to Happiness" is also close in theme to other Parnell poems in Pope's selection. "Thrice happy men! (or find a phrase / That speaks your bliss with greater praise)," is echoed in "And find a life of equal bliss" (A, 201, 99); and "E'en death, that seems to set them free, / But brings them closer still to thee" is echoed in "Shall only find by this decree / The soul flies sooner back to me" (A, 201, 90). The theme of this group of poems is, of course, highly conventional, a Christian reworking of Plato on the Highest Good, influentially expressed by Boethius and many other writers. What is interesting is Parnell's later improvement in expressing it.

The note of erotic mysticism is found in these shorter lyrics more clearly than in the Bible paraphrases. In "The Convert's Love" we hear of the "ravish'd soul" aspiring, of "fervent wishes" that say "I burn, I burn thy glorious face to see, / And live in endless joy with thee." Parnell writes that "There's no such ardent kind of flame / Between the lover and the dame" (A, 203) and uses the traditional Petrarchan love imagery of "pleasing pain." Just as this erotic mysticism has been seen as Catholic, so the poem "On Divine Love, by meditating on the Wounds of Christ" has been seen as revealing specifically Catholic tendencies. H. N. Fairchild writes that "Very few Queen Anne clergymen would dream of anything so popish as meditating on the Wounds of Christ. . . . In all the verses which have been quoted . . . one feels a Catholic spirit." Nevertheless, the tradition of emotional meditation on biblical scenes was also encouraged by Puritan writers, and, as H. Grant Sampson says, "The use of meditation and of its technique and style has long formed a part of the Anglican tradition."[16]

Certainly Parnell's poem on the wounds of Christ is a very clear example of the ancient meditative techniques—the "Composition of Place," the putting oneself mentally and visually before Christ in a particular situation or in a particular aspect, in this case Christ glorified in heaven, but with the marks of his passion still apparent. As Evelyn Underhill writes, ". . . the imaginative realization of the passion has always held a high place in the Christian devotional life."[17] What may be regarded as specifically Anglican about Parnell's poem, however, is the fact that he neither emphasizes the physical details of the wounds as might be thought more characteristic of Roman Catholic writings on the subject nor revels in an emotionalism that H. Grant Sampson regards as characteristic of evangelical and nonconformist meditation.[18] Parnell's version of Christ's wounds and blood is almost emblematic, almost purely symbolic—"Shed the precious purple tide / From thine hands, thy feet, thy side" (A, 213)—and the crucifixion itself an event seen from the perspective of the glorified Christ. The emotion that there is in the poem is presented in mystical not in sentimental terms. Further evidence that these religious poems are written from an Anglican perspective comes from references like those in "A Desire to Praise":

> To thee the churches here rejoice,
> The solemn organs aid the voice:
> To sacred roofs the sound we raise,
> The sacred roofs resound thy praise;
> And while our notes in one agree,
> O bless the church that sings to thee.
>   (A, 206)

Chapter Three
Occasional and Secular Poems

Most of the other secular poems by Parnell that are not included in Pope's collection are of small interest. Parnell's poem on the Peace of Utrecht, for example, was available to Pope, but he understandably chose to reject it. Banal in its phrasing, it makes much use of angels and overelaborate, yet trite personifications:

> In Flandria's soil, where camps have mark'd the plain,
> The fiend, impetuous Discord, fix'd her reign;
> A tent her royal seat. With full resort
> Stern shapes of horror throng'd her busy court,
> Blind Mischief, Ambush, close concealing Ire,
> Loud Threatenings, Ruin, arm'd with sword and fire,
> Assaulting Fierceness, Anger wanting breath,
> High reddening Rage, and various forms of death. . . .
>
> (A, 139)

Another of the longer occasional poems, "To Dr. Swift," is equally unsuccessful, though it is interesting to see that the earlier religiosity and the use of the idea of mystical rapture ("Rapt by the force of thought, and rais'd above, / Through Contemplation's airy fields I rove" [A, 129]) have been secularized and turned solely into a compliment to Swift's literary talents.

The handful of shorter secular poems not included by Pope that were published later in the eighteenth century include a moralistic fable on the evils of alcohol, "Bacchus; or, the Drunken Metamorphosis," and a good brief satire on the low-church Whig Bishop Burnet (who was attacked by all the Tory writers):

> For, as of late he meant to bless the age
> With flagrant prefaces of party rage,
> O'erwrought with passion, and the subject's weight,
> Lolling, he nodded in his elbow seat;

25

> Down fell the candle; grease and zeal conspire,
> Heat meets with heat, and pamphlets burn their sire.
>
> (A, 125)

The song "To a Young Lady on her Translation of the Story of
Phoebus and Daphne" was published as part of Steele's *Poetical
Miscellanies* and must therefore have been known to Pope. It is not
markedly inferior to the poems Pope did include and has a witty
epigrammatic polish to it. "On Mrs. Arabella Fermor leaving London" is also of interest, a polished piece of *vers de société* with that
typical post-Restoration polite realism about love:

> 'Tis constancy enough in love
> That nature's fairly shown:
> To search for more, will fruitless prove,
> Romances and the turtle-dove,
> The virtue boast alone.
>
> (A, 126)

Donne's Third Satire and Some Classical Poems

A poem that is definitely the result of Pope's influence is Parnell's
"translation" or "modernisation" of Donne's third satire. Pope himself attempted a version of Donne's second satire in 1713 at the
request of the Earl of Oxford and the Duke of Shrewsbury. He may
have asked Parnell to do the version of the finest of Donne's satires
because his own position as a Catholic made it embarrassing for
him to deal with the religious subject matter. The particular interest
of Parnell's version is in what it tells us of his stylistic aims at this
stage in his career. We see the aspiration toward balance, control,
and polish that is so evident in all the poems Pope selects for his
edition. In the version of Donne these qualities can be examined in
all the small details of technique.

The change of tone is apparent from the first lines. Donne's
violence and physical quality in "Kinde pitty chokes my spleene"
becomes Parnell's more decorous "Compassion checks my spleen."
The next significant change is in line 5, where Donne's reference
to "our Mistress faire Religion," presumably too blatant a sexual
image for Parnell, becomes instead the polite personification of
religion as a "Heaven-descended dame." Perhaps the most striking

example of the same tendency toward decorum is what happens to
the dramatic rise to a climax in Donne's lines:

> . . . and shall thy fathers spirit
> Meete blinde Philosophers in heaven, whose merit
> Of strict life may be imputed faith, and heare
> Thee, whom hee taught so easie wayes and neare
> To follow, damn'd?[1]

This is turned into the following balanced and regular couplets,
with the loss of a sense of climax and the transformation of "damn'd"
itself into a euphemism:

> And shall thy father's spirit meet the sight
> Of heathen sages cloth'd in heavenly light,
> Whose merit of strict life, severely suited
> To reason's dictates, may be faith imputed,
> Whilst thou, to whom he taught the nearer road
> Art ever banish'd from the blest abode?

> (A, 119)

Overall, Parnell turns Donne's poem into a work of what Donald
Davie calls "chaste diction."[2] In the early biblical poems Parnell
had been in danger of overelaborate attempts at the sublime on the
one hand and of naive simplicity on the other. The poems Pope
chooses for his edition have a greater sophistication and politeness
of tone. This reveals itself in a diction that is a mean between the
two extremes. As Pope put it, "As there is a difference between
simplicity and rusticity, so the expression of simple thoughts should
be plain but not clownish."[3]

In trying to achieve this effect Parnell loses much of the richness
of Donne's vocabulary. The startling metaphor, ". . . And dars't
thou lay / Thee in ships woodden Sepulchers" (lines 17–18) is flat-
tened into ". . . Or live entomb'd in ships" (A, 120). Words like
"salamanders" and "limbecks" are cut, of course, from Parnell's
version, but even the word "sentinell" (line 31) is replaced by the
commoner "sentry" (A, 120).

Much of the intensity and compression is also lost. Donne's poem
is 110 lines long, Parnell's 148. Donne writes, for example:

> Seeke true religion. O Where? Mirreus
> Thinking her unhous'd here, and fled from us,
> Seekes her at Rome; there, because hee doth knowe
> That shee was there a thousand yeares agoe.
>
> (lines 43–46)

Parnell's version is two lines longer:

> Seek thou religion primitively sound,
> Well, gentle friend, but where may she be found?
> By faith implicit blind Ignaro led
> Thinks the bright seraph from his country fled
> And seeks her seat at Rome, because we know,
> She there was seen a thousand years ago.
>
> (A, 121)

He loses the choppy colloquial use of the caesural pause in "O Where," adds "bright seraph" in a typical piece of early eighteenth-century piety, puts in the vocative "gentle friend" (an intimate Horatian note), and provides the Miltonic inversion of "faith implicit."

The most obvious changes that Parnell makes in his "versification" are in the direction of balance and anaphora. His couplets are, of course, much more regular and formal than Donne's. The roll of adjectives in "Plain, simple, sullen, yong; / Contemptuous, yet unhansome" (lines 51–52), is given in Parnell the well-known pattern of Denham's famous "Cooper's Hill" passage: "Though young, unhandsome; though unhandsome, proud" (A, 121). Donne's ". . . Those blest flowers that dwell / At the rough streames calm head" (lines 103-4) becomes "Each flower ordain'd the margins to adorn / Each native beauty, from its roots is torn" (A, 124). Overall, however, despite the qualities in Donne that Parnell has lost, he can at least be said to have made a neat and easily comprehensible version.

Parnell's desire for this neatness and control came partly, of course, from his sense of classical literature. Among the unpublished poems in Professor Rawson's possession are brief imitations of Horace, Martial, and Propertius. Two of the best unpublished poems are the translations of *The Battle of the Frogs and Mice* and "The Vigil of Venus," both of which are included by Pope. Two other poems published later in the century, "The Judgment of Paris" and "Elysium," are attractive re-creations of well-known classical themes and imitate Vergil and Ovid. "Elysium" in particular has some of the elegant, classically inspired nature description that is one of Parnell's most characteristic notes, and both have that air of elaborate Vergilian and Ovidian love melancholy that was cultivated in the period:

> These, and a thousand and a thousand more,
> With sacred rage recall the pangs they bore,
> Strike the deep dart afresh, and ask relief,
> Or soothe the wound with softening words of grief.
> At such a tide unheedful Love invades
> The dark recesses of the madding shades,
> Thro' long descent he fans the fogs around,
> His purple feathers as he flies resound:
> The nimble beauties, crowding all to gaze,
> Perceive the common troubler of their ease.
>
> (A, 148)

The heroic couplet is not used here with the precision of Parnell's best work. Yet there is an elegant and resonant effect, and the more exotic Latin tone of which Parnell is so fond is paradoxically one of the factors that has led critics to regard him as "preromantic."

Essay on the Different Styles of Poetry

The most important and ambitious poem of Parnell's that Pope omits is *An Essay on the Different Styles of Poetry*. This too is in the heroic couplet, and if there are imperfections in places, the meter is undeniably competent in general. Parnell's craftsmanship here helps to demonstrate that the good qualities of the poems Pope selects and corrects are not to be attributed solely to Pope's revisions. In fact, the main reason the *Essay* was not included by Pope appears to be its praise of Bolingbroke, in exile as a Jacobite by the time Pope's volume was published. Objections on these grounds by the poet's brother, Sir John Parnell, a respected lawyer, are the reason Swift gives for its excision from a Dublin text of Parnell's poems, and they are likely to have influenced Pope too.[4]

Prefaced to the *Essay* are some interesting comments on allegory, which will be examined further in the chapter on Parnell's prose. Parnell begins by explaining the basis of his allegory, the idea of wit as a Pegasus or winged horse that carries the poet through the differing landscapes of different kinds of poetry. One major source for the whole allegory is likely to have been Cowley's poem "The Muse." The tradition behind Parnell's poem is that of the verse essay on the poet's craft that began with Horace's *Ars Poetica,* continued with Vida and Boileau, and produced several English examples before Parnell, of which the most distinguished was Pope's *Essay on Criticism.*

The speaker in the poem is an ancient Greek poet, who describes the various styles of writing as if they were countries over which the young writer flies on wit, his Pegasus. The first is a brown land of labored conceits and puns, of acrostics and shape poems. The ideas here are taken primarily from Addison's discussions of false wit in the *Spectator.* The next region is a cold one of correctness without inspiration. Here several lines are especially reminiscent of Pope's *Essay on Criticism,* for example, "And drag in loitering numbers slowly by."[5] Then comes an open but low territory of conventional fancy and commonplaces, and it is contrasted with a land of violent rhetoric and the false sublime. Here we find that suspicion of the imagination attested in many places in the period and a similar sense of the potential dangers of the sublime to that which made Pope write *Peri-Bathous:*

> When writers rampant on Apollo call,
> And bid him enter and possess them all,
> And make his flames afford a wild pretence
> To keep them unrestrain'd by common sense.
> Ah, sacred Verse! lest Reason quit thy seat,
> Give none to such, or give a gentler heat.
>   (A, 173)

At last inspiration reaches the land of true poetry and the true sublime. Here the basis of the argument is Platonic, though Parnell reverses Plato in saying that the poet deals with the "Fair Ideas" which are the archetypes of Nature and are:

> Above the beauties, far above the show
> In which weak Nature dresses here below.
>   (A, 174)

In this beautiful realm of true poetry, fancy and judgment work in harness. Description and Narration are found at their best and all the nobler passions are aroused. The different figures of speech are

neatly arranged in this country too: for example, repetitions or turns
on words:

> These Repetitions one another meet,
> Expressly strong or languishingly sweet,
> And raise the sort of sentiment they please
> And urge the sort of sentiment they raise.
>
> (A, 179)

This technique stems ultimately from Vergil, Ovid, and other Latin
poets. It is an attempt to ornament and polish, and much use is
made of it in Parnell's own work. The poet also speaks interestingly
of the figure of speech called personification:

> There stand the new creations of the muse,
> Poetic Persons, whom the Writers use,
> Whene'er a cause magnificently great
> Would fix attention with peculiar weight.
>
> (A, 179)

Personifications were beginning to be particularly popular in the
poetry of this time. Addison devotes great attention to them. Their
fashionableness may be why Parnell calls them new. "New creations"
may, on the other hand, be a theological term to emphasize that
these imaginary beings are created directly out of the poet's mind,
not by immediate imitation of what already exists, as, theologically,
God Himself sometimes creates something completely new.

To this Palace of Art the great heroes of old and the great lovers
resort, and they are joined by the heroes of the present to live forever
in the songs of the poet. Bolingbroke, says Parnell, has given up
the pleasures of this realm to sacrifice himself for England. The
piece ends with a demonstration of the poet's power, in an idea
borrowed from Dryden's "Ode on St. Cecelia's Day," to rouse and
to delight by showing how a poem dealing with heroic exploits fires
a young man with emulation and how a poem of love inspires a
lady with compassion for her lover.

The overall structure of the allegory in this *Essay* is rather mechanical, but it is nevertheless an interesting poem. Parnell emphasizes the importance of wit, passion, and invention at the same
time as judgment, correctness, and reason and stresses that if wild
pseudosublimity is to be avoided, then so too is frigid correctness

or predictable cliché. What we find here is not so-called "prero-manticism," but a reminder that the preconceptions and norms of early eighteenth-century literature were far less narrow than was once thought. Pope too praises invention passionately in the preface to his *Iliad*. As R. S. Crane has shown, the set of literary norms called "neoclassicism" in fact involved holding values like imitation of the classics and correctness in tension with other values like originality. Parnell's *Essay* shows interestingly how this may be done.[6]

Unpublished Satires, Elegies, and Occasional Pieces

Among the previously unpublished work in Professor Rawson's possession is a variety of other secular verse, including several classical imitations, some Scriblerian epigrams, and a group of satires and "elegies,"[7] a word used to describe any formal lyric reflections, not just those on the topic of death. The formal verse satires are of particular interest in extending our sense of Parnell's range as a poet.

Several poems in this group concern the subject of poetry itself. The first contains brief comments on contemporary poets and suggests that the whole breed of poets are fools and madmen. This view is not of course intended to be taken with complete seriousness. It is a deliberately stock response, a development of a theme in Horace, but it does show the conventional reaction against that enthusiasm with which the wilder strains of poetry were linked. Another poem on verse is a more positive celebration of its power, its therapeutic function in the expression of passion in particular. "The Test of Poetry" is an interesting attack on the itch for publication in the period. Parnell comments on the immorality of some contemporary love poetry, but says that poetry must nevertheless be respected because prophets, saints, and angels had used it. The answer is not to be anxious to publish your poems, but to keep them for a long process of polishing and revision, as Horace had advised, for the exercise of judgment is as important as wit and fancy.

A less interesting group of these satires and elegies treats commonplace moral themes in a conventional way. One of the liveliest, a poem on virtue, asks the same question Swift asks in "Stella's Birthday, 1727" about what reality "virtue" can be said to possess.

A man-about-town argues that there is no such thing as virtue and that "Sporus" is chaste only because he is impotent, but his arguments are controverted by "Trueman." "The Picture of Time" is moralistic in the tritest way, describing our need for the guidance of reason. "The Court" is a conventional piece of anti-court satire and moral advice, saying that much impiety infects it and that it is a place of moral danger. It must never be forgotten, however, that the glorious Queen Anna inhabits it too. "The Pretty Gentleman" is an equally conventional satire of a young man-about-town, Damon, who is in debtors' prison. Two poems about love are also moralistic. In "The State of Love" the theme is the corruption of love in the modern world compared to the state of innocence in the golden age. In another comment on love a shepherd tells beauties to beware of their lovers' prattling tongues, for sincerity is rarely to be found among them.

The second satire in this group, "On Law," refers to the men of the Irish bar. The presence of this poem makes it likely that the whole group was written before Parnell's attention was completely dominated by the social world of London, that is, before about 1712–13. In other words this group of poems was written after the solemn biblical ones but before Parnell's closest contacts with the other Scriblerians. "The Isle of Wight," a poem about the Duke of Ormonde, would confirm this supposition since he replaced Marlborough as Commander of the British forces at the end of 1711.

Apart from the relatively organized and formal group of satires and elegies, several other unpublished poems in this collection are of interest. An intimate personal epistle to a friend advises him against spending too much time and energy on writing poetry and suggests that he devote himself instead to the law. A charming untitled poem written in a humorously colloquial style is addressed to fishwives and fruitsellers about the idea that Homer was born from one of their ancestors. A poem in a similar style anticipates or complements Gay's *The Shepherd's Week* in emphasizing that there is no Arcadia in the country and describing drunk and promiscuous country folk. For a full study of all these as yet unpublished poems it is obviously necessary to await Professor Rawson and F. P. Lock's forthcoming edition.

Chapter Four

Pope and the
Poems on Several Occasions

Parnell was deeply influenced by serious-minded Protestant traditions of biblical poetry and the biblical sublime. Within these
traditions he was inclined to write in an unconvincingly enthusiastic
style in which mystical rapture and flights of poetic inspiration went
together. He was also inclined to write shorter Christian pieces of
an unpleasingly artless simplicity. The literary evidence would seem
to suggest that the poems in both categories were early "apprentice"
work. There is no way of proving this absolutely, but Parnell's work
in these traditions is clearly distinct from the lighter, classically
oriented occasional verse that makes up the main contents of his
Poems on Several Occasions as edited by Pope. In what are surely his
most characteristic and influential poems, "A Hymn to Contentment," "A Night Piece on Death," and "The Hermit," the Christian
seriousness remains, but the presentation is controlled by a classical
sense of form and the tone has the same easy grace as the other
poems in Pope's volume.

Parnell has clearly been influenced by his contacts with the London
literary world. The classicism was itself part of his educational
background. The urbanity and wit perhaps were not. Addison and
Steele gave him the model of earnest Christian reformers who yet
remained very careful to be fashionable and stylish, to blend moral
instruction and even piety with graceful wit and ease of tone. In
Pope and Swift he met great writers who had preserved a wit that
more specifically related to that of the Restoration, and in the
Scriblerus Club he mixed freely with them and with aristocratic
politicians.

The Traditions of Polite Occasional Verse

Parnell's work as presented in Pope's volume is a fine example of
the tradition of early eighteenth-century polite verse, also seen at

its best in Matthew Prior and John Gay, and influencing Pope himself, as the preface to his 1717 volume shows. It is a tradition of the gentlemanly amateur, a restrained and perhaps more "middle rank" version of the poetry of the Restoration court wits. The early eighteenth-century poets in this tradition wrote for an audience that was still primarily upper class, though it might also include intelligentsia from "the Middling Gentry of a liberal Education" addressed by Ambrose Philips.[1] The readership for poetry was perhaps slightly larger than it had been at the Restoration. Certainly those groups that had traditionally read and bought poetry bought more of it now. The 1709 Copyright act gave writers greater bargaining powers with the booksellers, and John Gay received the unusually high sum of £1000 for a volume of his poems.

The sale of poetry in the early 1700s was still not large enough, however, to provide a living for poets. It was only Pope's particularly businesslike use of the subscription method that enabled him to support himself as a writer. Aristocratic canons of taste still dominated both poets and audience. Though the better poets sometimes wrote for political preferment or even in the hope of making money from sales, they shared old-fashioned aristocratic prejudices at the same time about being professionals.[2] Goldsmith later remarked enviously on the fact that Parnell was a poet by inclination, not by necessity.[3] These poets liked to imply that they would not have published had their friends not begged them to, though Pope made fun of the survival of this aristocratic convention in an age of commercialism when he talked of the Grub Street writer "oblig'd by hunger and request of friends."[4]

For these poets to publish under the title *Poems on Several Occasions* was to suggest that they wrote only "occasionally," as even Pope himself implied at times.[5] Parnell's earnest ant says that poets should "sing but seldom if they love to sing" (A, 79). The title *Poems on Several Occasions* was self-deprecating in some ways, suggesting the courtly nonchalance recommended by Castiglione, the Renaissance guide to court behavior. It therefore also involved the social pride of linking oneself with quasi-aristocratic traditions. The polite tone of these poets reflects their own sense of social status. Their work is characterized by urbanity and tact. They are self-consciously classical, and their response to nature is modeled on classical poetry and has something of a connoisseur's tone. In these ways they reflect the interests of their self-consciously gentlemanly audience and their especial sense of intimacy with it. They knew it to be relatively small and cohesive, sharing the same classical education and the same knowledge of the personalities and events of "the town." Since the growth of the London season almost all of those likely to buy poetry spent some time each year in London. The "Circle of Politeness," said Swift sarcastically, extended "no further than London and ten miles round."[6] For several decades, as Bertrand Bronson explains, a community existed that "knew all the by-ways and short-cuts of conversational interchange as well as a schoolboy knew his physical surroundings; and an art that can employ this intimacy of reference can convey abundant meaning on subjects proper to it with the greatest verbal economy."[7]

W. H. Auden explained that this knowledge of one's audience and sense of security about its tastes was a necessary condition for the production of good light verse.[8] As R. D. Havens pointed out, the late seventeenth- and early eighteenth-century verse in the volume known as *Dryden's Miscellany* has a lighter tone and displays a greater classical influence than the poems in Robert Dodsley's *Collection* in the middle of the eighteenth century.[9]

Toward the end of the seventeenth century a reaction against Restoration court wit had occurred. Sir Richard Blackmore, Daniel Defoe, and others associated wit with Restoration immorality.[10] Addison and Steele, and Pope in the *Essay on Criticism,* sprang to the defense of wit and tried to purify it from any libertine associations.[11] The lighthearted tone of the best poets of the period reveals their desire to retain aristocratic wit and nonchalance, provided they be suitably modified. These poets can indeed sound worldly and risqué at times, though there is less of this tone in Parnell than in Matthew Prior, for example. Nevertheless, the extension of the tradition to a circle wider than that of the court and the reaction against Restoration extremism make these later poets politer than the Restoration wits. They have a touch of sentimentalism as well as of conventional moralizing. Yet they continue to dislike too direct a didactic purpose, preferring wit and obliqueness where possible, and looking back to the way that Renaissance courtiers learned to sugar the pill of moral instruction for the prince.[12] A link continues to be made between pedestrian moralizing and the Protestant middle rank. As Pope says, "Some who grow dull religious straight commence, / And gain in morals what they lose in sense."[13]

In their aristocratic wit and nonchalance these poets were also avoiding the highest literary claims. They have something of an amateur's playful spirit. They know that epic and tragedy are the highest forms, but their own classicism is in some respects inhibiting. [14] They associate the longer forms with presumptuous modern attempts to emulate the ancients or with the efforts of professional writers for which occasional poets would not have time. They also link ambitious poetic aspirations with the Protestant enthusiasm of the false sublime, which the Restoration wits had associated with the excesses of the Civil War zealots: "Beware what spirit rages in your Breast; / For ten inspired ten thousand are possest."[15] Swift in particular continued this dislike of enthusiasm and condemned it through the ironies of the Digression on Madness in the *Tale of a Tub*. Pope's passionate dislike of the false sublime is shown especially in *Peri-Bathous*. The residue of the Restoration wit, skepticism and rationalism, courtly self-deprecation, religious and poetical prejudice, and dislike of professionalism—all contributed to this wariness about high flights in poetry.

The classicism of these poets leads them to retain mythological allusions, but in their sophisticated way they also burlesque mythology in a tone of teasing irony shared with their readers. Restoration skepticism and rationalism also led to a certain wariness and self-consciousness about fiction. An English translation of the Lockean Jean Le Clerc puts it unequivocally, saying that the reader must remember that he is about to read the "work of a Liar, who intends to entertain him with Fictions. . . . The poets are full of false thoughts, by which if we are not deceived yet we insensibly lose a good Taste and right Judgement."[16] It would be wrong to exaggerate the effect of these more extreme pronouncements. It would also be wrong to deny the existence of such a climate of opinion altogether.

Such pressures are clearly evident within the work of Parnell, Prior, Swift, Gay, and Pope. Against the false sublime and epic of Sir Richard Blackmore they oppose courtly wit. They write the light and social verse that their upper-class milieu encourages, though Parnell has first to reject the biblical paraphrases of his apprentice years. Sometimes they themselves hanker for epic high seriousness and the biblical sublime, as with Prior's *Solomon* or Pope's "Messiah." All of them are self-conscious about problems of fiction and reality, though they refuse to reject fiction altogether or to concede that it is incompatible with "truth." Yet Parnell has to tell his "Fairy Tale" in a detached way through the persona of his old nurse, and Prior and Gay and to a lesser extent Parnell play with the interrelationships between mythology, fictional conventions, and real life.

New attitudes toward love poetry are also apparent in reaction to Restoration excesses and in response to other changes of outlook.[17] The pervasive Restoration cynicism had itself had an effect, and Locke's influential empiricism is ultimately opposed to some of the mystique of the old Petrarchan love conventions. The growing moral respectability worked together with the gradual disaffiliation from a court culture. A new emphasis on directness, sincerity, and the "honest muse"[18] is apparent in love poetry, especially in the work of Prior and Swift. The minor poet, courtier, and politician William Walsh, for example, complained that the moderns filled their verses with thoughts that were "not tender, passionate or natural to a man in love."[19] At the same time the old hyperboles of Petrarchan love poetry were often retained, though they had by now lost much of their substance. They had been supplemented by the work of early seventeenth-century French writers on love, the *précieuses,* who had developed a very artificial diction and tone. As in the poems of George Granville, Lord Lansdowne, an important politician and a minor poet, who exercised considerable influence on Parnell,[20] the Petrarchan adoration of the lady was sentimentalized. The old conventions change into mere poetic diction, the "enchantment" of a woman in the old magical sense, for example, becoming the weakened modern "charm." Granville's cloying diction of "the fair" in all her charms, with her "resistless" eyes, surrounded by "the graces" and the "little loves," becomes pervasive, and the polite love poetry of the time displays either that tone or the new directness or, as with Parnell, an interesting interplay between the two.

What we call occasional poetry includes poems on personal events as well as on more public ones like treaties and marriages. The former are not in the public realm of high art in the fullest sense,[21] and the convention is, as we have seen, that they are not even intended for publication. So a degree of intimacy and sentiment comes to seem appropriate,[22] though of a self-conscious kind since there is a sense of the wider audiences too, and most of these poems were meant for publication despite the conventional disclaimer.

The influence of the French *précieuses,* the decline of some of the neoclassical inhibitions, and the change in love poetry were all part of the gradual development toward a new interest in sentiment. Literature had become less dominated by the court. As Lawrence Stone has shown, what he calls "affective individualism," an interest in private emotional sincerity and an affectionate family life, was growing throughout the period.[23] The Earl of Shaftesbury's philosophy was also increasingly influential, and it too put great emphasis on emotional response. All these trends are reflected in the work of the polite poets of the time. A controlled but genuine interest in emotional expression is evident, a curious combination of what seems like conventional sentiment with the sincerity of the "honest muse" and with witty playfulness. In Parnell more than in any other poet of the group these traits are also combined with what seems genuine religious emotion.

Parnell's *Poems on Several Occasions*

The poems of Parnell that Pope selected make up a typical early eighteenth-century miscellany of polished, witty, and classical verse, a compound of classical translations and original poems, love verses and fables, personal epistles, amusing occasional pieces, and a few serious moral poems. The volume begins with one of its lightest, most elegant pieces of *vers de société*, "Hesiod; or, The Rise of Woman," an account of the gods' creation of woman—Pandora, superlatively beautiful yet treacherous—as a punishment for man. The poem is dependent on its classical prototypes and allusions yet it is also a very characteristic early eighteenth-century piece in its teasing social satire and its use of the conventional diction of contemporary love poetry for ironic effect. Both subject matter and tone are similar to Gay's *The Fan* and Pope's *The Rape of the Lock:*

> To dress the maid the decent graces brought
> A robe in all the dyes of beauty wrought,
> And plac'd their boxes o'er a rich brocade
> Where pictur'd loves on every cover play'd;
> Then spread those implements that Vulcan's art
> Had fram'd to merit Cytherea's heart;
> Fine locks in golden chains for bracelets hung,
> Gay buckles sparkling round about the tongue,
> And brazen pins, a num'rous aid on earth,
> From whence new turns of fashion find a birth;

> But chief, the mirror, where the ravish'd maid
> Beholds and loves her own reflected shade.
>
> (A, 8, 217)

Three love lyrics follow, the first interesting in its attempt to combine the traditional love imagery with the newer directness and sincerity, so that the mistress might "Still an angel appear to each lover beside, / But still be a woman to you" (A, 15). The poem was once attributed to Pope, but exists in a longer autograph version addressed to Parnell's wife. The second lyric, disillusioned, but without the full Restoration bitterness, shows how the jealousy and spite that two beauties display about each other frees their lover from his attachment to them. The third love lyric is a simple and affectionate address that uses the nickname of the poet's wife, "Nancy."

Two poems called "anacreontics" come next. The anacreontic is a classical genre of lyric associated with the praise of love or of wine. Parnell's pair is intended to illustrate each topic and to give a moralistic twist to the conventional approach. The first is a spring description deriving from many similar examples in Latin poetry, in particular the "Pervigilium Veneris" or "Vigil of Venus," itself translated later in the volume. The poet describes the festival of the mating of the birds and ends with the moralistic conclusion that love should always be directed toward suitable partners rather than being a sigh for "souls averse." The second anacreontic is written with boisterous colloquial energy. It is a translation of a poem by the minor Italian neo-Latin writer Aurelius Augurellus.[24] It tells of a drinking party at a famous London tavern owned by the well-known comic actor Richard Estcourt. After initial good humor Bacchus, Comus, Love, and Jollity fall out. As with the preceding poem, the conventional significance of classical anacreontics is altered so that the poem moves not toward the praise of wine but to the warning:

> But part in time, whoever hear
> This our instructive song;
> For though such friendships may be dear,
> They can't continue long.
>
> (A, 24)

In treating the gods with less than reverence, however, and combining them with Parnell's well-known contemporaries it conveys its moral with pleasing lightheartedness.

"A Fairy Tale in the Ancient English Style" tells the story of how the deformed youth Edwin is healed by the fairies and how the reverse happens to his rival Sir Topaz.[25] The tradition of fairy poems had died out after Michael Drayton, Robert Herrick, and William Browne of Tavistock. Parnell's poem is a response to the first signs of a contemporary enthusiasm for ballads and a renewed interest in the "fairy way of writing." Addison wrote several essays in the *Spectator* in praise of ballads, and Nicholas Rowe also praised them in the prologue to *Jane Shore* in 1713. Dryden had briefly mentioned the "fairy way of writing," and Addison devoted another *Spectator* essay to that topic. He included fairy tales as one example of the especially creative kind of literature that concerns purely imaginary beings.[26]

Parnell deliberately attempts to imitate the archaisms and supernatural elements in the old ballads, and his poem is important in literary history as a very early example of the so-called ballad revival. Yet the tale is also a kind of fable, with the unmistakably clear moral characteristic of its period:

> But virtue can itself advance
> To what the favourite fools of chance
> By fortune seem'd design'd;
> Virtue can gain the odds of fate,
> And from itself shake off the weight
> Upon th' unworthy mind.
>
> (A, 32)

The Latin poem the "Pervigilium Veneris" ("Vigil of Venus") was written in honor of the spring festival of Venus, which lasted for three nights and celebrated love, generation, and the returning year. Once attributed to Catullus, its authorship is in fact unknown, and there is also controversy about its date, though it is certainly from the late classical period.[27]

What is significant about Parnell's attraction to this poem is that the original itself embodies what has been considered a "romantic" quality in Latin poetry of the late classical period, a definite eroticism

in love poetry, and a certain sensuousness in the description of
nature. Parnell's translation has the same tone as that regarded as
"preromantic" elsewhere in his work:

> Where meeting greens for arbours arch above,
> And mingling flowerets strew the scenes of love.
> ....
> Thus deep the swan begins, and deep the song
> Runs o'er the water where he sails along.
> ....
> How long in coming is my lovely spring?
>
> (A, 37, 42, 43)

A specifically eighteenth-century concern for correctness and elegance is also evident in Parnell's version. He makes considerable
use of the method of rhetorical repetition called anaphora in the
construction of his lines:

> Here dancing Ceres shakes her golden sheaves.
> Here Bacchus revels, deck'd with viny leaves:
> Here wit's enchanting God in laurel crown'd
> Wakes all the ravish'd Hours with silver sound.
> Ye fields, ye forests, own Dione's reign.
> And Delia, huntress Delia, shun the plain.
>
> (A, 38)

The sexuality of the source (". . . tomorrow the bride unashamed
will unfold from the wet cluster the crimson that lurked hid in its
taper sheath,")[28] is also given in translation a tone of Restoration
eroticism and gallantry:

> And she to-morrow weds; the sporting gale
> Unties her zone, she bursts the verdant veil;
> Through all her sweets the rifling lover flies,
> And as he breathes, her glowing fires arise.
>
> (A, 36)

As Wayland Hilton-Young has said in a critical study of translations
of the poem, Parnell's version overall is melodious and beautiful
even if it lacks something of the "direct freshness" of the original.[29]
   Very different in spirit is the other main classical translation in
Pope's volume, *The Battle of the Frogs and Mice*. The original is the

mock-heroic *Batrachomuomachia* once attributed to Homer. Parnell
uses George Chapman's translation and Samuel Parker's *Homer in a
Nutshell.* But Parker is more boisterous and irreverent than Parnell.
It has been shown that Parnell's work is closely related to Pope's
translation of Homer's *Iliad,* so that a specifically mock-heroic tone
is appropriate.[30] This note is certainly predominant in Parnell's
version from the very first lines:

> To fill my rising song with sacred fire,
> Ye tuneful Nine, ye sweet celestial quire!
> From Helicon's embowering height repair,
> Attend my labours, and reward my prayer.
> The dreadful toils of raging Mars I write,
> The springs of contest, and the fields of fight.
> How threatening mice advanc'd with warlike grace
> And wag'd dire combats with the croaking race.
> Not louder tumults shook Olympus' towers,
> When earth-born giants dar'd immortal powers.
> These equal acts an equal glory claim,
> And thus the Muse records the tale of fame.
>
> (A, 47)

Parnell's tone and cadences here have obviously been influenced
by *The Rape of the Lock,* and there are echoes of canto V, lines 45–
49 and 149. At the end of the poem he emphasizes that the whole
story makes up a miniature epic, a microcosm of the *Iliad:*

> But down Olympus to the western seas
> Far-shooting Phoebus drove with fainter rays;
> And a whole war (so Jove ordain'd) begun,
> Was fought, and ceas'd, in one revolving sun.
>
> (A, 66)

Parnell has been criticized for his retention of the Greek names of
his characters, but, as R. P. Bond points out, the elaborate-sounding
names like Cnissodioctes, a mouse "who follows the steam of kitch-
ens," are surely part of the mock-heroic intention.[31] In its lightness
of touch, considerable humor, and brilliant use of perspective the
poem is undoubtedly one of Parnell's best performances.

It is followed, appropriately enough, by a noble Horatian epistle
in praise of Pope, which says that before Pope's translation Homer

lay "in all the majesty of Greek retired" (A, 69). The connection with Pope himself continues with the translation of part of *The Rape of the Lock* into medieval Latin. The circumstances that lie behind this are discussed in the chapter on Parnell's life.

Marion K. Braggs in her study *The Formal Eclogue in England* attributes some historical importance to the next two poems, eighteenth-century versions of the classical eclogue or pastoral genre, "Health" and "The Flies." The first, an attractive celebration of the ideal of rural health, has a Greek model in a hymn to health by Ariphron of Sicyon, and is deliberately reminiscent of Milton's "L'Allegro." The second is a pleasant fable contrasting in traditional terms the vain and idle flies with the serious and industrious ants. Both poems contain sunny nature poetry. According to Professor Braggs, it is Parnell's infusion of the classical eclogue with a didactic quality that is his important innovation; but the teasing lightness of tone and detachment in "The Flies" must be remarked upon too.[32]

"An Elegy to an old Beauty" is another Horatian epistle, inspired probably by Horace's Ode 3.15, and by several English analogues, George Turbervilles's "To an Old Gentlewoman," Thomas Randolph's "To a Painted Mistress," Robert Herrick's "Upon Judith," Charles Montagu's "To the Countess Dowager of ———," and the Earl of Dorset's "Th' Antiquated Coquet." The address to the elderly lady who cannot give up vanity and flirtation contains a couplet on her pretty daughter that became proverbial, "And all that's madly wild or oddly gay, / We call it only pretty Fanny's way" (A, 81).

The next poem, "The Book-Worm," is a lively mock-heroic account of a pursuit of the insect through Parnell's library. It takes the opportunity for a good deal of literary satire on the writers who were the conventional targets of the Scriblerus club: Ambrose Philips, John Dennis, Thomas Shadwell, and others.

As the volume moves to its close a greater moral seriousness becomes evident. This note is first heard with "An Allegory on Man," Johnson's favorite among Parnell's poems. Based on a fable told by the Latin mythographer, Hyginus,[33] it presents an account of man's predicament, torn between heaven and earth, and dominated by Care. It reveals an unmistakable Christian moral seriousness at its close, but its octosyllabic meter and colloquial quality prevent too heavy-handed and solemn a tone even here:

> 'Tis well, said Jove; and for consent
> Thundering he shook the firmament:
> Our umpire Time shall have his way,
> With Care I let the creature stay.
> Let business vex him, avarice blind,
> Let doubt and knowledge rock his mind,
> Let error act, opinion speak,
> And want afflict, and sickness break,
> And anger burn, dejection chill,
> And joy distract, and sorrow kill:
> Till, arm'd by Care, and taught to mow,
> Time draws the long destructive blow;
> And wasted man, whose quick decay
> Comes hurrying on before his day,
> Shall only find by this decree,
> The soul flies sooner back to me.
>
> (A, 90)

As if to confirm the suspicion about too facile an expression of
poetic moralizing we find next "An Imitation of Some French Verses,"
a poem about the moral reflections and resolutions of a sick man
who changes them the moment he feels better:

> But hold—I feel my gout decrease,
> My troubles laid to rest,
> And truths, which would disturb my peace,
> Are painful truths at best.
>
> (A, 92)

This poem is symptomatic of what might be considered a worldly
and urbane side in Parnell. It was encouraged by his contacts with
the Scriblerus Club and helps to undercut the grave biblical solemnity of his earliest work.

Nevertheless, Pope's volume ends with three poems of considerable moral seriousness and strong Christian teaching: "A Night
Piece on Death," "A Hymn to Contentment," and "The Hermit."
Pope seems to have regarded it as appropriate that the volume should
rise gradually from the lightest *vers de société*, love lyrics, and anacreontics to Christian high seriousness at the close. These last three
poems, however, avoid the length and the extravagant tone of the
biblical sublime traditions. The "Hymn to Contentment" is much
more restrained than Parnell's other poems on similar themes, while

the "Night Piece" and "The Hermit" embody their moral teaching
in clear artistic structures and, in the case of the latter, in a neat
and formal narrative. They are remarkable for their brevity and
control. It is for these reasons that they appealed to Pope.

"Blest in Ev'ry Strain."

In his beautiful poem dedicating his volume to Harley, Lord
Oxford, Pope refers to Parnell's "tuneful tongue" and says that he
was "blest in ev'ry strain." The latter comment has been taken by
Geoffrey Tillotson to refer to Parnell's skill in versification and
mastery of different meters.[34] This seems a reasonable interpretation.
One intention behind Pope's selection seems to be to illustrate his
friend's command of different forms and different meters. As we
might expect, Parnell is certainly a master of the heroic couplet.
The teasingly intimate social tone of "Hesiod; or The Rise of
Woman," for example, is partly created by the conversational couplet, which can nevertheless rise to the righteous indignation of the
following:

> The days of whining court, the wild intrigues,
> Commenc'd or finish'd with the breach of leagues:
> The mean designs of well-dissembl'd love;
> The sordid matches never join'd above;
> Abroad, the labour, and at home the noise,
> (Man's double suffering for domestic joys;)
> Expense or fashions tho' the wealth decay,
> Tho' still we see the danger, fret and pay;
> The curse of jealousy, the curse of strife;
> Divorce, the public brand of shameful life;
> The rival's sword; the qualm that takes the fair;
> Disdain for passion, passion in despair. . . .
>   (A, 12, 218)

Parnell can create an enactive speed and energy with a quick succes-
sion of verbs of action:

> I mount the courser, call the deep-mouthed hounds;
> The fox, unkennell'd flies to covert grounds;
> I lead where stags through tangled thickets tread,
> And shake the saplings with the branching head;

> I make the falcons wing their airy way
> And soar to seize, or stooping strike their prey.
>
> ("Health," A, 75)

He can also achieve the stately splendor of the youth's transformation into an angel in "The Hermit":

> His youthful face grew more serenely sweet;
> His robe turn'd white, and flow'd upon his feet;
> Fair rounds of radiant points invest his hair;
> Celestial odours breathe through purpled air;
> And wings, whose colours glitter'd on the day,
> Wide at his back their gradual plumes display.
> The form ethereal bursts upon his sight,
> And moves in all the majesty of light.
>
> (A, 106)

Like Swift and Prior, Parnell also uses octosyllabics well. Of his fifty-eight published poems, twenty-eight are in the heroic couplet and sixteen in octosyllabics. This meter often helps to create the effect of a certain briskness, as with the "Allegory on Man," where the avoidance of undue solemnity of tone is part of his purpose. Parnell's range with this meter is in fact greater than Prior's and Swift's because they make little attempt at the "Il Penseroso" solemnity Parnell attains in the "Night Piece."

There is also a considerable variety of other meters—the vigorous attempt at something that might sound ballad-like and archaic in "A Fairy Tale," for example. This is an imitation of a common meter in medieval romances, the one Chaucer chose for parody in "Sir Thopas." Johnson was particularly impressed by the meter of "An Imitation of Some French Verses," and appreciatively quoted the first four lines:

> Relentless Time, destroying power,
> Which [*sic*] stone and brass obey,
> Who giv'st to every flying hour
> To work some new decay.
>
> (A, 91)

He comments that "Quatrains of lines alternately consisting of eight and six syllables make the most soft and pleasing of our lyric measures."[35]

Parnell undoubtedly has real lyric gifts, which are apparent in the poems in heroic couplets and octosyllabics as well as in those that would be regarded as lyrics in the technical sense. In the latter his command of stanzas is notable. Coleridge copied as one of his "metrical experiments"[36] the first stanza of the beautiful tripping rhythm and interwoven rhymes of the "Song":

> When thy beauty appears,
> In its graces and airs,
> All bright as an angel new dropt from the sky;
> At distance I gaze, and am aw'd by my fears,
> So strangely you dazzle my eye!
>
> (A, 15)

Pope's Revisions

Though there are good passages in the 1758 volume, the poems as a whole do not create the impression of polish and correctness. There are unhappy word choices and awkward versification in places. The poems in Pope's selection are more polished metrically and purer in diction than most of those he leaves out. Even in these poems, however, blemishes remain. Apart from the so-called "Irish rhymes" for which Parnell was attacked,[37] there are occasional infelicitous phrasings like "As harpers *better* by the loss of eyes" from "An Elegy to an Old Beauty" (A, 81). Even in "The Hermit," as G. A. Aitken shows, there are awkward phrasings and trite rhymes occasionally, as in "Far in a wild, unknown to public view, / From youth to age a reverend hermit *grew*" (A, lx, 106). Parnell was a genuinely occasional poet, unlike some of the others who adopted the pose. He was also notoriously dilatory. His proposed revision of *The Battle of the Frogs and Mice* delayed its publication despite the eagerness of Pope and was never completed. He gave Pope his manuscripts with authority to do what he wished because he trusted Pope's judgment more than his own and because of his own reluctance to undertake the process of revision.

It has occasionally been argued that Pope's revisions must have been numerous and far-reaching and that the qualities attributed to Parnell were really Pope's.[38] Full study of Pope's revisions must await the forthcoming critical edition. In 1755, however, appeared an edition of Parnell's *Works in Verse and Prose*,[39] which included what were claimed to be specimens of the original text of poems revised by Pope. Professor Rawson has established the validity of these variations, which were taken from original manuscript sources.[40] We also have the texts of the poems Steele published, which were revised by Pope in some places. The evidence thus provided does not substantiate the view that Pope's revisions were always an improvement of Parnell. It is debatable, for example, whether Pope's treatment of "The Bookworm," which he shortened by omitting the names of various writers, is a gain in brevity or a loss of topical vigor.

An occasional polishing and sharpening of effects is certainly noticeable. The previously quoted rhetorical listing in "Hesiod" of the ills man will experience from women builds up to a stronger climax in Pope because of the omission of the six-line simile in Parnell's manuscript:

> As men who sailing touch on Libyan land;
> See brinded Panthers scour the desart sand,
> Fierce Wolves and Tigers wand'ring swains engage,
> And scaly Dragons fill the realms with rage;
> If still the distant breaks are heard to roar
> Much what they view they dread and fear for more.
>
> (A, 218)

Pope is right to feel that this exotic, almost mock-heroic simile weakens the effect of the buildup and the climax,

> These, and a thousand, yet unnam'd we find,
> Ah fear the thousand, yet unnam'd behind.
>
> (A, 12)

On the other hand, as we shall see, Pope omits an important and beautiful simile near the end of "The Hermit," one that relates to the symmetry and even the themes of the whole poem. In several other poems he more forgivably omits descriptive similes from nature that have a certain beauty and pointedness, as when the hermit grows calmer and Parnell writes, "So loud through rocks the trembling waters stray, / Then glide beneath the fall unheard away" (A, 226).

The omission of similes is based on clear, if sometimes regrettable policy. Other omissions seem more arbitrary. In the account of the hermit's life at the beginning of the poem, for example, Pope omits for no apparent reason a couplet of Parnell's describing the hermit's possessions: "His goods a glass to measure human breath, / The books of wisdom, and the spade of death" (A, 224). At another place in "The Hermit" Pope deliberately seems to make Parnell's lines less specifically Christian in their doctrine and phrasing. Parnell had written:

> Eternal God the world's foundations laid;
> He made what is, and governs what he made.
> His sacred majesty through all depends
> On using second means to work his ends.
>
> (A, 226)

Pope alters this to:

> The maker justly claims that world he made,
> In this the right of Providence is laid,
> Its sacred majesty through all depends
> On using second means to work his ends.
>
> (A, 107)

No one would argue, presumably, that Pope's version is any great literary improvement on Parnell's. Its point must be understood to lie in a certain deistic tendency. The change helps to emphasize by contrast Parnell's own Christian purposes, but the speculations to which it gives rise have more to do with Pope than with Parnell, and need not be pursued further here. Enough has been said to show that it is far from always true that Pope's revisions are an improvement of Parnell. The available evidence does not appear to suggest that he ironed out many blemishes that would otherwise have appeared in these poems, or that he added essential qualities lacking in the original.[41]

Chapter Five
Poems on Several Occasions II: Literary Qualities

The poems of Parnell selected for Pope's edition have a greater sophistication than most of those printed elsewhere. They display brevity and wit and artistic control. Their tone has a certain urbanity and the diction avoids both the extravagance and the embarrassingly flat naiveté of the work that appeared in the *Posthumous Poems*. The qualities of elegance and polish have been described as "simplicity" by David Hume and as "purity of diction" by Donald Davie.[1] In neither case is something flatly direct, simple and pure in a primitivist sense, meant, but rather the purity produced by a careful honing of the language, a refining from false elaboration. Parnell's best poems have a literary tact that makes us conscious that he does not have to overdo any effect. This is in part a function of his improved sense of his audience. He shared the advantage of this firm sense of audience with other poets in his group, and the feeling that his audience perfectly understood him made it possible for him to avoid overinsistence.

Purity of Diction and the Polite Tone

The qualities of Parnell's best work are hard to analyze fully since they depend on the subtlest adjustments of tone: a matter of innuendo, allusion, delicacy. The very frequency with which critics mention such qualities speaks for itself, yet they must obviously be embodied in the texture and smallest details of the style. Certainly an examination of the diction in the poems Pope selected gives the impression that, despite occasional blemishes, Parnell has tried to choose the most lucid, most central word in the language, avoiding both vulgarity and overelaboration. They are poems in which, as Donald Davie says, the feeling is that "a selection has been made and is continually being made, that words are thrusting at the poem and being fended off from it." Parnell becomes "conversational, not colloquial, poetic not poetical. The effect is a valuable urbanity, a civilized moderation and elegance."[2]

Something of the way Parnell refines his diction in order to achieve the effects Davie describes has already been seen in the account of his modernization of Donne's third satire. Goldsmith criticized those contemporaries of his who "imagine that the more their writings are unlike prose, the more they resemble poetry" and declared that "from these affectations the poems [of Parnell] are entirely free; he considered the language of poetry as the language of life, and conveys the warmest thoughts in the simplest expression."[3] Parnell's best poems certainly base their diction on the polite language of good conversation. There are some signs in the classical translations of more elaborate poetic diction, but they are rare, and the purpose on these occasions is either to create the special quasi-scientific formality frequently sought in nature poetry in the period or else mock-heroic effects, as in *The Battle of the Frogs and Mice.* More usually the diction of Parnell's better poems remains simple and yet precise, natural and yet with a small but significant degree of elevation and formality.

This sense of formality is also created by the smoothness and polish of Parnell's versification, by the frequent rhetorical repetition and artificial ordering of the lines:

> For him the nymphs in green forsook the woods,
> For him the nymphs in blue forsook the floods.
>
> (A, 12)

Also pervasive is the Latinate device of the "turn," a repetition and play on words: "Which felt they curse, yet covet still to feel" (A,6). Parnell describes the use of these "turns," drawn especially from Vergil and Ovid, in his *Essay on the Different Styles of Poetry.* They create a feeling of ornamentation and elegance, of logical relationship, and even of epigrammatic wit, though often the manipulation is not much more than purely verbal.

More genuine wit is used to give substance to the relative plainness of Parnell's diction in a whole series of arch euphemisms and verbal ironies. This kind of euphemism is naturally a prevailing weakness in early eighteenth-century polite verse, as when Donne's "damn'd" becomes "Art ever banished from the blest abode" (A,119) in Parnell's modernization. But Parnell deliberately plays with euphemism, particularly in "Hesiod," to create an apparent coyness that becomes knowing and sophisticated, rather tongue-in-cheek, as in the references to nude statuary and to pregnancy: Pandora receives a robe "To copy Venus' air, / When Venus' statues have a robe to wear," and, after the lovers meet, "Swelling Nature in a fatal hour / Betray'd the secrets of the conscious bower" (A,9, 13). In the second quotation, with the Latinate sense "conscious," the bower itself is rather knowing, like the poet.

Small ironies are common in the poems in Pope's selection. The old lady in an "Elegy to an Old Beauty" is advised:

> Thy pendant diamonds let thy Fanny take,
> (Their trembling lustre shows how much you shake;)
> Or bid her wear thy necklace row'd with pearl,
> You'll find your Fanny an obedient girl.
>
> (A, 81)

The irony of the woman's adornments making her age even more obvious and the throwaway line, "You'll find your Fanny an obedient girl" create a knowing intimacy with the reader. There is a more disturbing irony in "A Night Piece on Death" about the graves of the "middle race of mortals," with whom Parnell obviously links his readers by the use of the possessive pronoun:

> The flat smooth stones that bear a name,
> The chisel's slender help to fame,
> Which e'er our set of friends decay
> Their frequent steps may wear away.
>
> (A, 94)

It is the visits of our friends who wish to commemorate us that in fact destroy our only physical memorial.

All the verbal devices and figures of speech Parnell uses are more restrained in Pope's selection. In the other works, as we have seen, personification is often very extravagant and elaborate, an unconvincing attempt at sublimity. In the Pope volume personification is always neat, and it can have a slightly ironic tone, like the picture from the "Allegory on Man" of "A thoughtful being, long and spare, / Our race of mortals call him care," or the humorous picture of Mother Earth, "who trail'd a landskip-painted vest" (A,87, 88). The best example is the masterly personification of sloth as a society lady with the vapors, living in splenetic luxury, in "Health, An Eclogue": "Let Sloth lie soft'ning till high noon in down / Or lolling fan her in the sultry town" (A,75).

Parnell's relationships with Addison and Steele and then with Pope, Swift, and the Scriblerus Club sharpened his sense of audience, and the improvement in the tone of his poetry is remarkable. Addison and Steele in their periodical essays were especially concerned to form the tastes of their readers, and they needed to create a special relationship with them in order to persuade and manipulate them. In the Scriblerus Club interchanges Parnell experienced an intimacy and ease combined with wit and intellectual vivacity that he was able to transfer to his poetry. Donald Davie refers to the "exquisite assurance, the confident communication between poet and reader which dignifies the slightest pieces of Thomas Carew or Thomas Parnell."[4] What this depends upon is a mastery of diction and convention and a strong sense both of the immediate recipient of the poem and of the wider polite audience.

The two songs at the beginning of Pope's collection, "Thyrsis, a young and amorous swain" and "My Days have been so wond'rous free," show a deliberate contrast in diction, convention, and relationship with the reader. The second is simple in diction and attempts to create the effect of simplicity, "O teach a young, unpractis'd heart, / To make my Nancy mine." The audience is imagined as overhearing the wooing, since the poem is addressed primarily to "Nancy," the poet's future wife. The pastoral diction of the first song is used with deliberate sophistication. Shepherdesses are traditionally innocent and artless. The fact that these are so spiteful builds an irony into the very use of the pastoral. Parnell sets up a relationship with his audience that implies that they share a worldly and knowing quality, so that they feel above Thyrsis's "fond romance" and are not surprised at his disillusionment:

> He haunts the stream, he haunts the grove,
> Where'er the friendly rivals rove,
> Lives in a fond romance of love,
> And seems for each to die;
> Till each a little spiteful grown,
> Sabina Caelia's shape ran down
> And she Sabina's eye.

> Their envy made the shepherd find
> Those eyes, which love could only blind;
> Thus both the chains of love unbind,
> So set the lover free:
> No more he haunts the grove or stream,
> The flowery walk of either dame,
> Or with a true-love knot and name
> Engraves a wounded tree.
>
> (A, 16, 219)

This sense of an audience appears to be lacking in the *Posthumous Poems*. There Parnell preaches or confesses with no apparent relationship to an addressee. The poems in Pope's volume often have a particular recipient in mind as well as the general reader. This is frequently the effect in volumes called *Poems on Several Occasions* where the convention is the old aristocratic one of the "stigma of print," the idea that these are poems addressed privately, not intended for publication and only printed therefore at the later request of friends. Parnell was an amateur poet, and he genuinely conveys this sense of intimacy with the immediate recipients of his poems. Even the poems addressed to fictional recipients imitate the real social intimacy of poems like "To Mr. Pope." The tone is carefully adjusted in all these poems to suit the original addressee, but the wider gentlemanly audience is given the privilege of being drawn into the poet's circle of friends, and the emotional warmth and ease of the primary relationship spills over onto them too.

In several poems the question of the relationship with the addressee is of paramount importance. "To Mr. Pope," for example, is partly about how to find the appropriate tone with which to address a famous public poet who is also a close personal friend. Its real subject is the strategy of praise and correct address. Only in a period with such a great concern with decorum and social life would a discussion of the proper tone for such a poem itself become one of the poem's main subjects:

> To praise, yet still with due respect to praise,
> A bard triumphant in immortal bays,
> The learn'd to show, the sensible commend,
> Yet still preserve the province of the friend.
>
> (A, 67)

"An Elegy to an old Beauty" concerns itself with an even more difficult problem of politeness and social tone. This is a moment in which, as Parnell puts it, "truth in spite of manners" must be told. Parnell has to find a relatively tactful way of reminding the elderly coquette to act her age and come to the recognition that "Why, really fifty-five is something old." He softens the blow through the use of the seasonal imagery. If there is winter in her face now, there had nevertheless been summer once:

> And once, since envy's dead before you die,
> The women own, you play'd a sparkling eye,
> Taught the light foot a modish little trip,
> And pouted with the prettiest purple lip.
>   (A, 80)

The compliments soften the harshness of the didactic note. The woman is foolish to resist the natural process, implied in the seasonal imagery, which will also certainly affect in turn the daughter of whom she is jealous. Parnell's poem remains gentler than its analogues like Dorset's "The Antiquated Coquet." He has managed to tell the truth without offending too much against manners.

One of Parnell's finest poems, "Hesiod, or The Rise of Woman," depends for its whole effect on its brilliant establishment of a tone of teasing intimacy with its audience. It alters mythology to make it not so much Pandora's box as Pandora herself, the first woman, that is the source of man's punishment. Yet the satire on womankind is ironically concealed. The ostensible point of the poem is to show through the fate of Hesiod himself, killed by two jealous brothers in mistake for their sister's lover, what punishment awaits poets who defame woman:

> Here Hesiod lies: ye future bards, beware
> How far your moral tales incense the fair:
> Unlov'd, unloving 'twas his fate to bleed;
> Without his quiver Cupid caus'd the deed:
> He judg'd the turn of malice justly due,
> And Hesiod died for joys he never knew.
>   (A, 14)

In fact, the poem is full of the conventional complimentary diction of "charms" and "the fair" as well as of polite euphemisms. It becomes an example of that teasing "raillery" and that oblique satire that was especially valued in the period.[5] It is a sly mixture of flattery and satire of womankind. Parnell puts the whole burden of the attack on women on the classical poet, enabling himself to remain ironically noncommittal. He also establishes a special tone of social intimacy by giving the impression of writing specifically for a female audience. At the same time he flatters his sophisticated readers by implying that they can see through the irony:

> In Greece they fram'd the tale;
> In Greece, 'twas thought a woman could be frail.
> Ye modern beauties! where the poet drew
> His softest pencil, think he dreamt of you,
> And warn'd by him, ye wanton pens, beware
> How heaven's concerned to vindicate the fair.
> The case was Hesiod's; he the fable writ;
> Some think with meaning, some with idle wit:
> Perhaps 'tis either, as the ladies please;
> I wave the contest, and commence the lays.
>
> (A, 5)

The playful manipulation of mythology contributes to this tone, and the poem becomes the quintessence of Parnell's polite, teasing social verse.

Classicism and Nature Poetry

In an important article already mentioned R. D. Havens points out that a greater classical influence and more humor and lightness of touch distinguish the best early eighteenth-century poetry from the best work of the mid-century.[6] These are the signs of the continuation of an aristocratic bias in taste. We can see them working together in the poems Pope selected. Goldsmith wrote that Parnell "was the last of that great school that had modelled itself upon the ancients."[7] Parnell's classicism is evident both in the longer translations and in the classical allusions in the shorter original poems, which serve to elevate the subject matter and give it associations of beauty and dignity: "Now friends conversing my soft hours refine / And Tully's Tusculum revives in mine" (76). Parnell's education obviously gave him a strong grounding in the classics. In the 1758 volume the preponderance of the poems are nevertheless in the

biblical sublime traditions. Most of the poems Pope selected have
classical prototypes and classical overtones. Parnell's classicism has
modulated into the distinctively early eighteenth-century gentlemanly kind. He has learnt, for example, a tone of light burlesque,
which was especially popular with Gay, Swift, and Matthew Prior.
It suggests an affectionate knowledge, shared with the reader, of
much-loved works and the sense that these tales from classical mythology are not factually true and can be played with by writers and
readers sophisticated enough both to love and to disbelieve them.
This is the note, for example, of the anacreontic "Gay Bacchus
liking Estcourt's wine," where the classical figures are irreverently
treated and blended with well-known contemporary figures.

Parnell has also learnt a distinctively classical and polite nature
poetry. Goldsmith especially praised him for his elegant and classical
selectivity in his criticism of nature: "To copy nature is a task the
most bungling workman is able to execute; to select such parts as
contribute to delight, is reserved only for those whom accident has
blest with uncommon talents, or such as have read the ancients with
indefatigable industry."[8] This is similar to Hume's view that "nothing can please persons of taste, but Nature drawn with all her graces
and ornaments, 'la belle nature,' " and Parnell is one of Hume's
examples.[9]

Such an approach seems more appropriate than the attempt to
class Parnell as an original descriptive poet or a preromantic. "Descriptio" was one major element in an epic poem, according to Le
Bossu.[10] The Neoplatonic element in description is apparent in *An
Essay on the Different Styles of Poetry*. "Description" dwells above "the
show / In which weak Nature dresses here below" (A, 174), though
it utilizes the beauty of the actual world. The central image remains
that of painting:

> Here bold Description paints the walls within,
> Her pencil touches, and the world is seen;
> . . . .
> The skies, extended in an open view,
> Appear a lofty distant arch of blue,
> In which Description stains the painted bow,
> Or thickens clouds, and feathers-out the snows,

> Or mingles blushes in the morning ray,
> Or gilds the noon, or turns an evening gray.
>
> (A, 176)

Parnell is attracted by what could be considered the more "romantic" aspects of Latin poetry, the loves and the moonlit woods of "The Vigil of Venus," for example. His diction remains literary, echoing and alluding to English translations of classical poetry as well as original English poetry, and using stock words like "azure" and "gilded" for the sky, "painted" for the plumage of birds, and "silken pinions" for wings. The point of drawing on this stock diction is to achieve a musical elegance, dignity, and assurance on these subjects. The allusive diction reminds readers of poetic descriptions that have pleased them in the past and puts Parnell in the same poetic tradition. The description of evening in "The Hermit," for example, "Now sunk the sun; the closing hour of day / Came onward, mantled o'er with sober gray" (A, 101) echoes Milton's "Now came still evening on, and twilight gray / Had in her sober livery all things clad."[11]

The emphasis of these nature descriptions is usually generalizing:

> High sunny summits, deeply shaded dales,
> Thick mossy banks, and flowery winding vales,
> With various prospect gratify the sight
> And scatter fix'd attention in delight.
>
> (A, 75)

The approach is that of a gentleman gardener: "For her I mow my walks, I plat my bowers, / Clip my low hedges, and support my flow'rs" (A,76). "Prospect" in the previous quotation is a word especially appropriated in poetry and in landscape gardening, and the same vocabulary from landscape gardening is used in "The Hermit."

The nature descriptions are not purely stock responses, however. At times, as with diction like "the finny crew" and "the feathered nation" ("Vigil of Venus," A,33, 34), the idea is an attempt at a quasi-scientific categorization of the different species and thus the hope of being both general and precise. Usually there is enough detail to prevent it all from being purely conventional, vague, and literary. But Parnell's own individual responses are not regarded as relevant as such. The element of art is often deliberately stressed. The word "piece" meant a painting in the early seventeenth century, and the "Night Piece" is meant to have the quality of a painting: "How deep yon azure dyes the sky."[12] Parnell consciously directs the eyes of the reader from aspect to aspect of the view:

> The lake is smooth and clear beneath,
> Where once again the spangled show
> Descends to meet our eyes below.
> The grounds which on the right aspire,
> In dimness from the view retire:
> The left presents a place of graves
> Whose wall the silent water laves.
> That steeple guides thy doubtful sight
> Among the livid gleams of night.
>
> (A, 93)

The description here is just particularized enough to evoke the reader's own responses to such scenes on previous occasions as well as to previous literary descriptions and paintings. We observe the poet's elegant selectivity at work. He manages to seem fresh and yet elegantly conventional at the same time.

Sometimes Parnell creates allegorical landscapes where the conventionality of the description is in a sense the point: these are ideal landscapes, symbolic representations of the world of art, and their beauties are bound to be those of nature abstracted and idealized. The best example of this technique of allegorical landscape is "To Mr. Pope," where Parnell re-creates the landscape of Arcadia to symbolize the world of Vergil's and Pope's art:

> Parent of flowerets, old Arcadia, hail!
> Here in the cool my limbs at ease I spread,
> Here let thy poplars whisper o'er my head;
> Still slide thy waters soft among the trees,
> Thy aspens quiver in a breathing breeze;
> Smile all thy valleys in eternal spring,
> Be hush'd, ye winds! while Pope and Virgil sing.
>
> (A, 68)

He then contrasts this movingly with the Irish landscape, which comes to symbolize intellectual barrenness and Parnell's melancholy feeling of exile:

> For fortune plac'd me in unfertile ground;
> Far from the joys that with my soul agree,
> From wit, from learning—far, o far from thee!
> Here moss-grown trees expand the smallest leaf,
> Here half an acre's corn is half a sheaf;
> Here hills with naked heads the tempest meet,
> Rocks at their side, and torrents at their feet;
> Or lazy lakes, unconscious of a flood,
> Whose dull brown Naiads ever sleep in mud.
>
> (A, 70)

The full-scale allegorical landscape of the *Essay on the Different Styles of Poetry* lacks the pointedness of the description in "To Mr. Pope," where the drop from the conventional language of the idealized landscape to realism is powerful, but then the actual landscape is suddenly and wittily fused with the conventions in "dull brown Naiads." The melancholy is relieved by irony and wit, and the conventions permit subtle parodic effects that would not otherwise be possible.

A final element in Parnell's nature poetry is the survival of traces of seventeenth-century religious lyricism about nature, the tradition of Andrew Marvell and Henry Vaughan. Parnell's octosyllabic couplets are sometimes reminiscent of such seventeeth-century predecessors, as in the "Hymn to Contentment." Usually, however, Parnell's attitude to nature in such contexts is less powerfully numinous that in his models.

Allegory, Miniaturism, and Detachment

Addison had recently displayed an interest in allegory because of its imaginative and fictional qualities. Parnell says in the preface to his *Essay on the Different Styles of Poetry* that allegory could also be "one way of preserving us from writing without schemes" (C,9:413). In the biblical paraphrases and other early poems he had sometimes abused the idea of using allegorical personages, like the angel of piety in "Piety, or the Vision." He fails to prepare for such an extravagant device and often makes too close a connection between such personages and himself. In the poems Pope selected these faults are overcome. In "A Night Piece," for example, Death appears halfway through the poem, after tone and atmosphere have gradually prepared us for it.

Parnell by this time has grown toward a greater classical control and artistic impersonality. The religious or other sentiment found in many of the poems not selected by Pope, the artless and naive emotionalism of some of the hymns, for example, is now chastened. Parnell's best verse is able to retain something of this sentiment but combine it charmingly with a marked formality and control. The effect of the rhetoric now is not that of an overelaborate attempt at heightening emotion but the opposite, the channeling and formalizing of it. It is the combination of a certain artlessness carried over from the apprentice poems with evident artistic polish, of an obvious personal sincerity with a deliberately emphasized conventionalism that has fascinated readers. It is not in fact always easy to distinguish the genuine naiveté found in some places from the deliberate cultivation of sentiment elsewhere. Parnell's sentiment is certainly sometimes itself made conventional, polished, and refined, in order to appeal to the taste of his readers.

Overall, he has learnt how to produce a poetic artifact without losing the impression of emotional freshness. In the biblical paraphrases he frequently intruded with apostrophes to his fancy or with lamentations on his own sinfulness. Now the specifically personal note is more likely to come in at the end, as in the lines in "To Mr. Pope" on his exile in Ireland. He has learnt the artistic advantages of detachment and irony. He several times makes use of the third-person spokesman in order to remain ironically noncommittal himself, as in "Hesiod, or the Rise of Woman" or "A Fairy Tale in the Ancient English Style."

The latter poem has been seen as an early example of the exploration of the mystique and the romantic quality of the world of fairy. Something of this is indeed present:

> As there he bides, it so befell,
> The wind came rustling down a dell,
> A shaking seiz'd the wall:
> Up spring the tapers as before,
> The fairies bragly foot the floor,

> And musick fills the hall.
> ....
> With that Sir Topaz, hapless youth!
> In accents faultering ay for ruth
> Intreats them pity graunt;
> For als he been a mister wight
> Betray'd by wandering in the night
> To tread the circled haunt.
>
> (A, 30)

Addison had made it clear, however, in his influential recommendation of "the fairy way of writing," that poets and audiences were meant to keep a distance from such stories too: "Besides this he [the poet] ought to be very well versed in legends and Fables, antiquated Romances, and the Traditions of Nurses and old Women, that he may fall in with our natural prejudices, and humour those Notions which we have imbibed in our Infancy."[13] This is the case with Parnell's poem. Though it is a remarkably early example of the interest in ballads and the use of archaisms, the archaism is not there solely to add glamour, but to assist the poet's distancing from the story, attributed to his old nurse: "This tale a Sybil-Nurse read; / She softly strok'd my youngling head" (A,31). The attribution to a third-person speaker permits the preservation of skeptical detachment at the same time as an enjoyment of the "fairy way of writing." In the poem's moral and in the distance it keeps from its own fictions it is more typical of its period than might at first appear.

In the *Posthumous Poems* a title like "An Allegory on Man" would have portended a heavy-handed poem in the biblical sublime tradition. Now, however, Parnell uses "Jove" as a surrogate for the Christian God and embodies the moral in an objective narrative. He writes in a brisk octosyllabic meter and with a racy colloquialism that gives a real energy to the dramatic interchanges between these personified figures. Instead of the solemnity and heavy-handedness of the *Posthumous Poems* we appreciate the brevity and lightness of touch here:

> Halves, more than halves! cried honest Care,
> Your pleas would make your titles fair,
> You claim the body, you the soul,
> But I who join'd them, claim the whole.

....
As thus they wrangl'd, Time came by.
(A, 88–89)

In "Piety, or The Vision" the angel had given Parnell the unfortunate advice, "Be thy Muse thy zeal." Now the poet has learnt
the more aristocratic approach to poetic morality, the courtly ideal
of *Sprezzatura* or graceful ease, a certain distancing from and obliqueness in his didactic or Christian purposes. Clearly enough, this is
the result of his contacts first with Addison and Steele and then
with his Scriblerus Club friends.

In this context Parnell is also particularly fond of miniaturist
effects, an interest he shared with the other Scriblerian poets. This
relates partly to the fashionable enthusiasm for optics, telescopes,
and microscopes in the period. In poetry in particular, short pieces
are linked with the craftmanship required to make something beautiful out of a small subject. Thomas Yalden's "The Insect Against
Bulk" (1693) is almost a manifesto in these terms: "In a small space
the more perfection's shown, / And what is exquisite in little's
shown."[14] Richard Lovelace's "The Ant" is an early example, and
appears to have influenced Parnell's "The Flies, An Eclogue." Pope's
sylphs in *The Rape of the Lock* show the impulse at its finest.

Parnell himself can create wonderful poetry out of tiny creatures.
In *The Battle of the Frogs and Mice* he uses mock-heroic diction very
cleverly in this respect, referring, for example, to cats as "the potent
warriors of the tabby vest" because we are seeing everything from
the perspective of the mice. From the same perspective the crabs
become a horrifying apparition:

Strong suits of armour round their bodies close,
Which, like thick anvils, blunt the force of blows;
In wheeling marches turn'd, oblique they go;
With harpy claws their limbs divide below;
Fell sheers the passage to their mouth command;
From out the flesh their bones by nature stand;
Broad spread their backs, their shining shoulders rise;
Unnumber'd joints distort their lengthened thighs.
....
On eight long feet the wond'rous warriors tread;
And either end alike supplies a head.
These, mortal wits to call the crabs agree,
The gods have other names for things than we.
(A, 65–66)

The magnifying technique often also creates a tone of polite wit, an amusement at the tiny creatures shared with the reader. In Parnell's best work the connoisseur's interest in minute effects takes the form of a kind of pathetic fallacy, the attribution of feeling to a part of nature normally regarded as incapable of it. This is blended with a mock-heroic tone too. A fern or a blade of grass is given sympathy and at the same time made slightly ridiculous. We find this technique even in "The Gift of Poetry" from the 1758 volume:

> The tender blades of grass, when beams diffuse,
> Rise from the presence of their early dews,
> Point towards the skies their elevated spires,
> And proudly flourish in their green attires.
>
> (C, 9:373)

Here the pathos and humor come from "elevated spires," which makes us think of cathedrals rather than blades of grass, though it is appropriate to both, and from "proudly flourish." There is a similar later passage in "The Flies":

> There stands a slender fern's aspiring shade
> Whose answering branches, regularly laid,
> Put forth their answering boughs, and proudly rise
> Three stories upward, in the nether skies.
>
> (A,73)

As Donald Davie has explained, Parnell deliberately turns his back here on the evidence of the senses, calling the stalk and stems of a fern "branches" and "boughs," which we think of as massive. Yet there is the logic of analogy behind this too. It is not purely fanciful. With the Latinate "aspire" and "proudly" a note of pathos is added to the mildly grotesque element of mock-heroic.[15] The blend of sentiment and wit that results is very characteristic of Parnell.

In this poem the flies in the ludicrousness of their adoption of the pose of lovers are particularly intended as a puncturing of contemporary affectations and poeticizing:

> So, when a stage invites to pageant shows,
> If great and small are like, appear the beaux.

In boxes some with spruce pretension sit.
. . . .
These gentle tunes and whining songs forebear,
Your trees and whispering breeze, your grove and love,
Your Cupid's quiver, and his mother's dove.
Let bards to business bend their vigorous wing,
And sing but seldom, if they love to sing.

(A,77, 79)

The miniaturism gives a special lightness of touch to the moral of
the fable. The ant spokesman is described in mock-heroic terms,
though what he says probably has Parnell's support:

Yet one grave sage a moment's space attends,
And the small city's loftiest point ascends,
Wipes the salt dew that trickles down his face,
And then harangues them with the gravest grace.

(A,79)

In this case, though, it seems as if the shared amusement at the
incongruity of these tiny creatures loving and moralizing is more
important than the conventional moral.

Parnell has grown toward an easy grace and wit and a distaste
for some aspects of that "zeal" the angel recommended to him in
"Piety." He practices mock-heroic and a light burlesque of the
classics. He distances himself from his moral purposes by the use
of third-person spokesmen. He embodies his ideas in economical
narratives and allegories and puts his moral teaching in the mouth
of the comic little creatures of the fables. He laughs urbanely in
"An Imitation of some French Verses" at the moral philosopher who
rejects the world in sickness but goes back to it when well. Frequently the apparent moral purposes themselves seem blunted, a
mere bow to convention, almost a part of the game, as with "The
Flies." This is far from always the case, however, as we shall see
with "A Night Piece" and "The Hermit."

Chapter Six

Poems on Several Occasions III: "A Hymn to Contentment," "A Night Piece on Death," and "The Hermit"

Pope ends his selection of Parnell's poems with "A Night Piece on Death," "A Hymn to Contentment," and "The Hermit." All three have a Christian seriousness and solemnity of tone, and it was appropriate, in Pope's view, that the volume should rise to this height. They later became Parnell's most famous and influential poems, and they have been praised as innovative, especially imaginative, and even as preromantic works. In each, however, I shall argue, Christian purposes are primary, and the sentiment that later poets and readers found so attractive was largely derived from these Christian purposes rather than cultivated for its own sake.

"A Hymn to Contentment"

"A Hymn to Contentment" has an obvious place in the long tradition of the search for the *Summum Bonum* or Highest Good, which stems back to Plato. Horace's extraordinarily influential poems on the theme of the "happy man" had been given a Christian form by the seventeenth-century Polish Jesuit poet Cassimire Sarbiewski. A similar reworking of the tradition by Cardinal Bona has been seen as a direct source of Parnell's poem.[1] But there were likely in fact to have been various English intermediaries, both translations of Cassimire and original poems like George Herbert's "Peace." Particularly close to Parnell in their rendition of the theme are two poems both called "Content" by the minor seventeenth-century poets Joseph Beaumont and Robert Fletcher. Lady Winchelsea's "Petition for an absolute Retreat" is also similar in theme and approach.

It is clear from its publishing history that the "Hymn" was written before Pope's intimacy with Parnell began. This means that it is likely to have been one of the earliest written poems to be included in Pope's selection. Various poems omitted by Pope are on the same theme, "On Happiness in this Life," for example, first published in the *Posthumous Poems.* This however, is insistently personal and inclined to melodrama in its tone—"And I moan upon the naked plain"—as well as to absurd apostrophes like "Return my senses" (A, 208). Parnell's "Hymn" is more obviously Horatian and far more controlled. Yet its conclusion has the same ideal of the vocation to the life of an inspired biblical poet of praise as in the apprentice poems:

> Might I thus my soul employ,
> With sense of gratitude and joy!
> Rais'd as ancient prophets were,
> In heavenly vision, praise and prayer.
>
> (A, 99)

Furthermore, it borders in places on the same naiveté of tone:

> All of these and all I see,
> Should be sung, and sung by me.
>
> (A, 99)

The poem is obviously thus a transitional one in Parnell's development. It first appeared in Steele's *Poetical Miscellanies,* and the influence of Addison and Steele's attempt to unite religion with politeness is apparent. Its relative stylishness and polished finish differentiate it from Parnell's other poems on the topic and made it acceptable to Pope.

Parnell begins with a beautiful apostrophe to Contentment and Peace of Mind:

> Lovely, lasting peace of mind!
> Sweet delight of human kind!
> Heavenly-born, and bred on high,
> To crown the favourites of the sky
> With more of happiness below,

> Than victors in a triumph know!
> Whither, O whither art thou fled,
> To lay thy meek, contented head!
>
> (A, 97)

He has gracefully blended together a variety of traditional ideas and phrases here. A similar apostrophe to peace is found as early as Barnaby Barnes's "Ah sweet content, where is thy mild abode?" Behind the whole idea are echoes of the Canticles, and there is similar phrasing in one of Francis Quarles's paraphrases of Job. Line seven is borrowed directly from Herbert's "The Search." The phrasing also recalls Lady Winchelsea's "Inquiry after Peace" and "To the Echo" and Nahum Tate's "The Search," and John Hughes had begun a paraphrase of Horace's Ode 2.16 in 1679 with an apostrophe to "Indulgent Quiet."[2]

In accordance with the tradition Parnell next runs through the different sources of false happiness, like avarice and ambition. He also rejects the pleasures of a melancholy like that described in Milton's "Il Penseroso" and seems to agree with John Evelyn's arguments about the dangers of rural solitude:[3]

> The silent heart which grief assails,
> Treads soft and lonesome o'er the vales,
> Sees daisies open, rivers run,
> And seeks, as I have vainly done,
> Amusing thought; but learns to know
> That solitude's the nurse of woe.
>
> (A, 97–98)

Parnell's support for what might be regarded as the more Augustan side in the debate about rural solitude and his emphasis on the futility of the pleasures of nature without God should in themselves have been sufficient to differentiate him from Wordsworthian or other romantic ideas, despite the claims of later critics. We notice too that in this poem he begins with the generalizing statements and only then moves to the personal comment, "As I have vainly done."

Parnell also stresses the inadequacy of the scientific and in particular the astronomical search for truth. Vergil's famous lines in the *Georgics* about the blissful contemplation of the heavens and the search for the causes of things had been taken up by Newton's followers.[4] The influence of Newton's work both strengthened and altered the traditional attitudes toward finding God in nature. The great scientist was seen as having established the presence of natural laws in the universe that proved the existence of a benign and ordering Creator. The whole emphasis of late seventeenth- and early eighteenth-century theology in Britain was on these natural scientific proofs of God, concentrated especially in the works of the so-called "physico-theologians."[5]

Though a Newtonian and physico-theological emphasis can be found later in the poem, Parnell is careful at this point to emphasize in the most orthodox terms that the study of nature in itself avails nothing:

> To range the circuit of the sky,
> Converse with stars above, and know
> All nature in its forms below;
> The rest it seeks, in seeking dies,
> And doubts at last, for knowledge, rise.
>
> (A, 99)

Instead he presents the need for God's grace, symbolized in the appearance of "the grace" Contentment in the poem. Indeed, because this apparition is the precise symbol of the theological truth Parnell wishes to convey, it is more impressive than most of his other uses of angelic or allegorical visitants. It occurs halfway through the poem, not at the beginning as in "Piety," and the yearning quest for Contentment has prepared us for it. The tone is one of evocative understatement, not baroque elaboration and splendor:

> The branches whisper as they wav'd:
> It seem'd as all the quiet place
> Confess'd the presence of the Grace.
>
> (A, 98)

What Contentment urges is ascetic self-control. The passions have to be purified before God and nature can be enjoyed, and this is the root of contentment. Parnell is writing here within the mystical traditions that regard the way of purgation as the necessary prelude to the ways of illumination and union.[6] In this respect, certainly, the poem is more seventeenth-century in its outlook than most other contemporary poems on similar themes. It rejects the enjoyment of nature, rural retirement, the pleasures of melancholy, and the aspirations of science inasmuch as they do not depend on God's grace.

With the presence of grace, however, and prepared by ascetic purgation, the poet can reach true contentment, a kind of spiritual ecstasy, "Pleas'd and bless'd with God alone." Moreover, this sense of God will also lead, as with Henry Vaughan and Andrew Marvell, to a renewal of joy in nature:

> The while the gardens take my sight
> With all the colours of delight;
> While silver waters glide along,
> To please my ear, and court my song;
> I'll lift my voice, and tune my string,
> And thee, great source of nature, sing.
>
> (A, 99)

As in Lady Winchelsea's work, Parnell's octosyllabic couplet here preserves something of a seventeenth-century religious lyricism about nature.

The emphasis on God as the "great source of nature," however, has more of the tone of the new century, and connections with Addison's influential Newtonian hymn "The Spacious Firmament on high" have been noted.[7] Addison had written that the heavens "Their great original proclaim." It is in this respect accurate to say that the poem could only have been written after Newton and that it reveals a physico-theological nature enthusiasm. As in Addison's "Hymn," the beauties of nature proclaim God, but since there is no longer any belief in the old tradition of the music of the spheres, they "speak their maker as they can." The poet's role in praising God thus becomes crucial, since nature is in this sense silent and wants and asks "the tongue of man." But if there are obvious interconnections between the survivals of seventeenth-century lyricism, Newtonian attitudes, and the later romanticism, it is nevertheless absurd to attribute romantic attitudes as such to Parnell and to his age-old emphasis on the need for Christian asceticism, which is much more scrupulously affirmed than in the work of most of his contemporaries.

"A Night Piece on Death"

Like the "Hymn," "A Night Piece on Death" and "The Hermit" also seem to stem from the period when Addison was the dominant influence on Parnell. In that they reveal fewer traces of naiveté these poems should probably be dated slightly later than the "Hymn" itself, however, and they would surely have appeared along with it in Steele's *Poetical Miscellanies* if they had been written by that time. Their Christian piety is far from tepid but, like Addison's, it has a public, rhetorical, and demonstrative quality. From a purely literary point of view the controls on Parnell's early fervor are an unmitigated improvement. In their polish and neatness of structure, their link between Christianity and the avoidance of impolite excess, and their concern for order all three poems express a specifically neoclassical form of Christian sentiment. They are all richly representative of their period, despite the exaggerated claims that have been made for their originality and preromantic qualities.

Such claims have above all been made for "A Night Piece." H. H. Clark, for example, wrote that Parnell "restored melancholy to literature"; P. van Tieghem argued that the "romantic" elements in "A Night Piece" were essentially an innovation;[8] and H. G. de Maar declared that the "Night Piece" was the "first 'Churchyard' poem of the eighteenth century."[9] All this appears to be based on a misunderstanding of Parnell's purposes. The innovative aspect of the poem have been much exaggerated. In a scholarly study of the concept of melancholy Amy L. Reed made the point that "I found to my surprise that the more closely I inspected 'romantic beginnings' such as, for instance, Parnell's 'Night Piece on Death,' the more readily they resolved themselves into elements thoroughly familiar to readers of the preceding century . . . ."[10]

It is certainly true that Parnell's poem is profoundly eclectic, and it is impossible to determine the exact degree of influence that the different traditions exercised on it. In a broad sense Parnell is using and contributing to the whole Christian and classical tradition of the "memento mori" or reminder of the inevitability of death and the idea that "The fear of death confounds me," as the Office for the Dead puts it. This emphasis is checked within the poem by the stronger Christian tradition of the hope of resurrection and hence by the sense of "Death, where is thy sting?" and Donne's assertion, "Death, thou shalt die!"

In more specifically literary terms there were several well-established traditions of meditation on death. In one way, for example, Parnell continues the genre of midnight meditations on death that stemmed ultimately from Macrobius's commentary on Cicero's "Dream of Scipio." William Drummond of Hawthornden wrote an influential prose piece in this tradition called "A Midnight Trance" (later revived as "The Cypresse Grove"). Henry Vaughan also wrote the prose "Man in Darkness; or a Discourse on Death."[11] Edward Arwaker's pastoral poem "The Birth-Night" of 1705 seems to be a poetic version of some aspects of this tradition.[12] In its night emphasis this tradition blended with other literary night descriptions, and the influence of Milton's "Il Penseroso" is above all apparent. As Louis Martz has shown in *The Poetry of Meditation,* a more general tradition of poetic meditations on death also existed, which was especially developed among the metaphysical poets.[13] In *The Funeral Elegy and the Rise of English Romanticism* J. W. Draper surveys the elaborate tradition of gloomy and melodramatic puritan elegies, which often described churchyards and churchyard scenes in detail. He adduces no concrete evidence that this tradition consciously influenced Parnell, but it is likely to have been a background presence.[14]

The "memento mori" and funeral elegy motifs blended easily in seventeenth-century poetry with reminiscences of Jacobean tragedy. Specific graveyard allusions occur, as in Thomas Flatman's "A Doomsday Thought": "Go to the dull churchyard and see / Those hillocks of mortalitie," or Nahum Tate's "Melancholy": "Through Charnel Houses then I'm led / Those gloomy mansions of the dead."[15]

As Draper shows, however, the optimistic Christian view of death was the basic Anglican tradition, both in verse and in prose, throughout the seventeenth century. Even the metaphysical poets, famous for what has been called their "metaphysical shudder" about death, more commonly ask "Death, where is thy sting?" and stress the resurrection. The poem called "Death" by the minor seventeenth-century poet William Hammond is a typical example of an ecstatic account of heavenly bliss. In the early eighteenth century John Pomfret's "A Prospect of Death" similarly emphasizes the hope of resurrection, as does the high Anglican Bishop Ken's "Preparations for Death."[16]

Meanwhile, prose works on the four last things, death, judgment, heaven, and hell continued to be very popular. One of the best

sellers, Dr. Sherlock's *Practical Discourse Concerning Death*, was highly
influential during the period before Parnell wrote his "Night Piece,"
and it continues the tradition of Christian cheerfulness about death,
the ultimate emphasis of Parnell's poem.[17] Sherlock's work was much
approved of by the *Spectator* writers. Religious melancholy as such
is condemned in numbers 494, 497, and 513. Addison himself is
the most influential exponent in the period of a hopeful and cheerful
Christianity. All these different traditions and strands, some biblical
or liturgical, some literary and some popular, are fused in the harmonious octosyllabic meter and polished finish of "A Night Piece."

The poem begins with a picture of the solitary poet "by the blue
taper's trembling light." As is often the case with Parnell, the first
few lines are a tissue of conventions and literary reminiscences.
Parnell presents himself as an "Il Penseroso" figure,[18] studying the
philosophers with his "lamp at midnight hour." The "trembling
light" of his taper is a literary commonplace, found in Donne's "The
Apparition," for example, as well as a traditional emblem of man's
life, so easily snuffed out by death. In Marvell's *Last Instructions to
a Painter*, as in Shakespeare's *Richard III*, the blue light itself suggests
the presence of ghosts. The actual phrasing of Parnell's lines is a
close echo of William Congreve's "To a Candle: Elegy."[19]

In a version of the old theme of experience versus authority as
well as of the "memento mori" tradition the poet rejects the sages
for the true wisdom to be found in the graveyard. After a fine
description of the night sky and the actual graveyard scene the poet
expresses the conventional sentiment evoked by the sight of the
graves: "Time was, like thee they life possest / And time shall be,
that thou shalt rest" (A, 94). He then gives an account of the
different classes of graves, those of the poor, those of the "middle
race of mortals," and those of the rich and great. At this stage,
halfway through the poem and in the midst of the churchyard, the
atmosphere is at its most ominous, the moon fades, and the poet
has a vision of the shades rising, "All slow and wan and wrapp'd
with shrouds."

Everything has now been prepared for the appearance of Death
himself at this climactic moment of tension:

> Now from yon black and funeral yew,
> That bathes the charnel-house with dew,
> Methinks I hear a voice begin;

> (Ye ravens, cease your croaking din,
> Ye tolling clocks, no time resound
> O'er the long lake and midnight ground!)
> It sends a peal of hollow groans
> Thus speaking from among the bones.
>
> (A, 95)

Clearly Parnell intends to frighten his readers at this point. The forceful reminder of death and its terrors is part of his Christian purposes. The melodramatic apparatus is a complex drawn from a wide range of possible antecedents, Isaiah, Vergil, Shakespeare, and various seventeenth-century predecessors among others.[20] But these terrors are evoked only so that they may be calmed. In a remarkable stroke of wit, in which Parnell was partly anticipated by William Drummond of Hawthornden,[21] the spokesman for the consolation is made the figure of Death himself.

Parnell's poem can thus certainly not be accused of the "emotionally-tinged religious attitudinising" of his successors.[22] What Death says is crucial to the poem and ignored by most commentators. The extravagant gloom that later writers like Robert Blair take up, as well as all the trappings of man's paraphernalia of death, are criticized within the poem by Death himself:

> Fools! if you less provok'd your fears
> No more my spectre form appears.

The horrors of death are really the creation of man:

> When men my scythe and darts supply,
> How great a king of fears am I!
> They view me like the last of things;
> They make, and then they dread my stings.

For the Christian, death need hold no fears:

> Death's but a path that must be trod,
> If man would ever pass to God.
>
> (A, 95)

The poem, in other words, is turning ironically back on itself, and its author, in a sense, criticizes the trappings of his own "graveyard poetry." Death himself rebukes all this melodrama by the criteria of polite moderation, recommending a gentlemanly Christian cheerfulness like Addison's. Those in the period and later who class Parnell with Edward Young and James Hervey and Robert Blair have failed to see what is going on. Far from being a preromantic poem, the "Night Piece" criticizes excessive emotion about death as being both impolite and unchristian.

The brief controversy about the meter is also relevant here. Goldsmith, reflecting a later and heavier Augustanism, complained that the poem was not in the heroic couplet and that octosyllabics were "very improper for the solemnity of the subject."[23] In fact, Parnell uses the meter with an impressive "Il Penseroso" solemnity in the first half of the poem, but there is also a lightness and speed at times compared to the heroic couplet in its heavier moods and certainly compared to the uncontrolled blank verse extravagance of Blair's *The Grave*. This brisker quality is particularly to be remarked upon toward the end of Death's speech. It is one major factor contributing to the brevity and control of the whole poem.

In comparison with Blair and indeed with Parnell's own longer biblical sublime poems "A Night Piece" provides yet more evidence of Parnell's new sense of restraint and of structure. The Christian consolation is skillfully prepared. The order behind all is suggested in anticipation through the beautifully ordered peace of the night sky.

> How deep yon azure dyes the sky,
> Where orbs of gold unnumber'd lie,
> While through their ranks in silver pride,
> The nether crescent seems to glide.
>
> (A, 93)

It is only the fears and pomps of man that disturb this order. For the Christian the disturbance is not final. The poem in fact moves superbly from real and symbolic darkness to the daylight of the resurrection:

> See the glad scene unfolding wide,
> Clap the glad wing, and tower away,
> And mingle with the blaze of day.
>
> (A, 96)

Like all of Parnell's best work "A Night Piece" is a poem of inspired conventionalism. Different traditional elements are smoothly blended and given the stamp of an individual re-creation and re-alization. The poem carefully keeps the fear of death in check and indeed criticizes it by Christian criteria at the close. As Professor Fairchild says, Parnell's sentiment has not been divorced from his genuine grasp of Christian truths.[24] However, the polished and harmonious expression that he gave to even the subordinate elements in his scheme meant that the cruder impulses that lay in the background of the poem were also helped to pass into the mainstream of respectable literary tradition. Some of these became attractive to successors less firmly rooted in Christian devotionalism, who put them in the forefront of their own work. "A Night Piece on Death" became a very influential poem, as we shall see, though later poets radically altered its proportions and significance.

"The Hermit"

"The Hermit" has a theme of portentous importance. It consti-tutes a miniature theodicy, a justification of the ways of God to men and a consideration of the whole problem of evil. In its elements of what H. N. Fairchild calls its "Whiggish didacticism"[25] it could obviously have been the subject of one of the overelaborate sublime poems that Pope did not include. Parnell has retained his interest in religious moralizing. Here, however, the moral is presented through the medium of a neat yet suspenseful narrative, and the more primitive elements in the sources of the tale are made elegantly acceptable to an eighteenth-century audience in ways Pope obviously approved of.

Some of the techniques Parnell uses in order to achieve these effects are analyzed in an excellent article on the analogues and sources of Parnell's poem by A. P. Hudson.[26] The hermit story in its basic form was used by an interesting range of writers. It appears, for example, in the *Gesta Romanorum* ("Deeds of the Romans," ca. 1326), which was translated into English in 1703, and in the *Divine Dialogues* of the Cambridge Platonist, Dr. Henry More (1614–1687). It was also readily available in James Howell's *Letters* and Sir Percy Herbert's *Certaine Conceptions* (1652).[27] According to Hudson, More's version is likely to have been the immediate source. He indicates that even compared with this version already refined from the crudity of the basic form the advantages are all on the side of Parnell.

Another background to "The Hermit" is the whole question of the theodicy or justification of the ways of God. Parnell's great early mentor, William King, Archbishop of Dublin, was the author of a major theological study of the topic, *De Origine Mali* ("Of the Origin of Evil," 1702).[28] Pope's interest in the matter is, of course, evident in his *Essay on Man*. More important, probably, as immediate influences on "The Hermit" are several theodicies on a more popular level, sometimes incorporating narratives, to be found in the *Spectator:* no. 483, 13 September 1712, for example, by Addison. no. 237, 1 December 1711, either by Addison or by John Hughes, is another discussion of the topic, which is especially close to Parnell's theme:

From hence it is, that the Reason of the Inquisitive has so long been exercised with Difficulties, in accounting for the promiscuous Distribution of Good and Evil to the Virtuous and the wicked in this world. From hence come all these Pathetical Complaints of so many Tragical Events, which happen to the Wise and the Good, and of such surprising Prosperity, which is often the Lot of the Guilty and the Foolish; that Reason is sometimes puzzled, and at a loss what to pronounce upon so mysterious a Dispensation.[29]

The essay ends with a brief tale from a Jewish tradition about Moses, which is very similar to "The Hermit." From a high mountain Moses watches a series of events. A soldier drops a purse of gold, which is picked up by a young boy. The boy leaves, and then an old man comes to the place. Not believing the old man's protestations, the soldier kills him. Moses is horrified, but God vindicates His providence and His justice by revealing to him that the old man was the murderer of the boy's father.

Parnell's poem begins with a description of the peaceful and solitary life of the hermit. Only the briefest external trappings, borrowed, it seems, from Spenser and Milton (*The Fairie Queene*, 1.1.305, for example, and "Il Penseroso," line 169), are sketched in, and the romanticizing of the life of retirement is slight. It is the religious note that is primary:

> Far in a wild, unknown to public view,
> From youth to age a reverend hermit grew;
> The moss his bed, the cave his humble cell,
> His food the fruits, his drink the crystal well,

His goods a glass to measure human breath,
The books of wisdom, and the spade of death.
Remote from man, with God he passed the days,
Prayer all his business, all his pleasure praise.

(A, 100, 224)

The peace is disturbed by a doubt which one day crosses the hermit's mind about the reality of God's providence. His ignorance of the world from actual experience is total. He resolves to leave his cell and explore the world looking for a solution:

To clear this doubt, to know the world by sight,
To find if books, or swains, report it right,
(For yet by swains alone the world he knew) . . .

(A, 100)

This last line has been criticized for an inconsistency. In Boswell's words, "as the Hermit's notions of the world were formed from the reports both of books and swains, he could not justly be said to know by swains alone." Johnson agrees that there is a contradiction, but there have been various attempts at an explanation. Some scholars have said, for example, that the word "alone" in the second line has no reference back to books but means swains as distinguished from all other persons. On the whole the attempts at justification remain unconvincing.[30]

In the aftermath of the first day of what is represented as the hermit's pilgrimage for truth he meets a good-looking young man and they agree to travel together. At night they seek shelter in a palace where they are lavishly entertained. After their departure the next morning the hermit is horrified to find that the young man has stolen a golden goblet from the host. On the second day a storm drives them to seek shelter from a churlish miser. The young man, much to the hermit's surprise, presents the miser with the stolen cup. On the third day they obtain lodging in the house of a man who appears to live in accordance with the golden mean and who is the epitome of hospitality. In the morning before they depart the young man strangles the only child of their host. The horrified hermit seeks to flee his companion, but does not succeed. On their way the young man also drowns one of the host's servants, who was acting as a guide. The old man's rage can now no longer be contained, but before he can say anything the young man is revealed before the hermit's eyes as a heavenly angel. He then explains the providential significance of all that has occurred. The loss of the golden cup has converted the first host from his vain ostentation, while its gift to the miser has shown him how heaven will reward him for even a little kindness on his part. The child was killed because the last host doted so much on him that it took him away from God, and so "God to save the father took the son" (A, 108). The servant who was drowned was false to his master and had intended to steal his treasure that night. After this explanation the angel ascends, and the hermit, his doubts about God's providence now completely resolved, returns to his "life of piety and peace" (A, 109).

As this summary makes clear, the poem raises philosophical and theological issues that it cannot entirely solve, and a certain crudity is built into the very structure of the old story that Parnell borrowed. Nevertheless, what he makes of it is remarkable. His poem is both polished and suspenseful. The shock of the scene in which the youth strangles the infant is intensified by the description of the idyllically peaceful family life that precedes. The description of the young man is itself skillful. His angelic identity is concealed from the reader in the interests of suspense and a dramatic dénouement. His beauty predisposes the hermit in his favor, makes the shock of his murderous behavior greater in contrast, and yet also makes the revelation of his supernatural quality more credible. The increase of suspense compared with Parnell's sources is not, however, simply in the interests of writing a good story. It relates to the theological purposes of the poem also, making the reader share the hermit's doubts and the satisfaction of their unraveling. Parnell's desire for polish and elegance is more than a mere eighteenth-century fashion too. It makes its own contribution to the theological import of the poem, as we shall see.

Overall, Parnell achieves a good balance between narrative and reflection, action and description. Setting and atmosphere are, as A. P. Hudson says, "just what they should be, no more and no less. There is in them just enough of restraint to keep them from being too romantic for a moral tale, and just enough of color and feeling to humanize the story."[31]

It is noteworthy that Parnell softens the harshness of the source material in places. He makes the angel say, for example, that the death of the infant appeared to the family to be from natural causes rather than from visible external violence. As Hudson also points out, in almost all the other versions the angel's motive for giving the miser the expensive cup is a cruel one. In Henry More's *Divine Dialogues,* for example, the angel gives it "as a plague and a scourge to the harsh inhospitable man that he might fall into intemperance."[32] Parnell's version is refined and touched with eighteenth-century sentiment:

> With him I left the cup to teach his mind
> That heaven can bless if mortals can be kind,
> Conscious of wanting worth, he views the bowl
> And feels compassion touch his grateful soul.
>   (A, 108)

Parnell's diction in "The Hermit" is pure in Donald Davie's sense, with many monosyllabic words, but given substance by "turns" and by a real precision of wording:

> Slow creaking turns the door with jealous care,
> And half he welcomes in the shivering pair . . .
>   (A, 103)

This precision is more than purely verbal. The polished simplicity of the style has a moral dimension. It enacts the avoidance of extremes that is part of the poem's moral message, the excess of passion like the father's for the child the angel kills, or the extravagant ostentation of the spendthrift's "vain flourish of expensive ease." The degrees of excess are conveyed through the verbal exactness:

> And all is more than hospitably good.
> ....
> Rich luscious wine a golden goblet grac'd,
> Which the kind master forc'd the guests to taste.
>   (A, 102)

Parnell also shows restraint in the use of baroque and sublime diction. The description of the angel comes from Cowley's description of Gabriel in the *Davideis,* but it is tactfully reserved till the final revelation, when the "form ethereal bursts upon his sight, / And moves in all the majesty of light."[33]

A clear and elegant symmetry is central to the style of "The Hermit," and it is created primarily by the formality of the couplet:

> Thus stands an aged elm in ivy bound,
> Thus youthful ivy clasps an elm around.
>
> (A, 101)

Such symmetry is also central to the poem's structure as a whole. The hermit is pious and faithful, then doubting, then pious again; he leaves his cell at the beginning and returns at the end; the youth seems godly at first, then morally monstrous, then again more godly than he at first appeared; the hosts behave in a way that seems to deserve a certain reward, apparently receive the opposite, and then are shown to have received their deserts all the time.

The elegant descriptions of nature contribute markedly to this effect of symmetry. The whole story is put in a polite eighteenth-century context, and Parnell uses the technical vocabulary of the landscape gardening of the period:

> At length 'tis morn, and at the dawn of day
> Along the wide canals the zephyrs play.
> Fresh o'er the gay parterres the breezes creep . . .
>
> (A, 102)

("Parterres" are ornamental slopes and the word "canals" also means a landscape-gardening feature at this time.) The descriptions of the time of day serve to underline the rhythm of the action. They also relate to the formal and moral pattern of the poem, not only to create a pleasing aesthetic object, but also to point out God's providential patterning of the whole universe, the poem's theme. These formal descriptions serve to indicate the way God arranges nature for man's benefit. A helpful perspective on this aspect of "The Hermit" is provided by a passage from "The Gift of Poetry: Moses," where Parnell emphasizes how God cares for man, the animals, and the whole of nature through the cycles of day and night and of the seasons. He talks of the birds who: ". . . by Gods appointment in their nest / With green surrounded, lie secure of rest," and of man, who:

> . . . next succeeding, from the sweet repose
> Of downy beds, to work appointed goes.

When first the Morning sees the rising Sun,
He sees their labours both at once begun;
And Night returning with its starry train,
Perceives their labours done at once again.
O! Manifold in works supremely wise,
How well thy gracious store the world supplies!
How all thy creatures on thy goodness call,
And that bestows a due support for all!
....
Thus, as you've seen th' effect reveal the cause,
Is Nature's ruler known in Nature's laws.

(C, 384–85)

This passage is dependent on the Psalms, especially Psalm 104, and on Tertullian and Boethius as well as Milton; Newton's influence is also apparent in the stress on "Nature's laws."[34]

The same kind of effect in small is intended in the nature descriptions in "The Hermit." There is a stress on the providential purpose of the cycle:

Now sunk the sun, the closing hour of day
Came onward, mantled o'er with sober gray;
Nature in silence bid the world repose . . .

(A, 101)

The continuation of this cycle of labor and renewal is emphasized throughout the whole poem: "At length the world, renew'd by calm repose, / Was strong for toil, the dappled morn arose" (A, 105). The strong sense of the pattern of dawn and evening, good weather and bad, is intended to suggest that the alternations of the action from good to bad and back again are also natural, and must be accepted as part of a providential rhythm making for man's good.

Pope unfortunately cut a simile describing the young man's revelation of himself as an angel that would have underlined this connection between natural description and theme. It is intended to remind the reader of the earlier storm after which the sun appeared, and it helps to unify the whole poem:

So when the sun his dazzling splendour shrouds,
Yet just begins to break the veiling clouds;

A bright effulgence at the first is seen,
But shorn of beams, and with a mist between
Soon the full glory bursts upon the sight
And moves in all the majesty of light.

(A, 226)

A connection is made between the ordered symmetry of the poem
and God's ordered universe. Parnell's ordered style here ultimately
has a metaphysical dimension. These lines refer back to the literal
storm followed by sunshine, but they are also semi-allegorical. The
sun behind the clouds suggests God's hidden providence. The angel
revealed in brightness like the sun breaking through clouds thus
becomes the manifestation of this providence in its fullness. Near
the beginning of the poem is an image of nature calmly reflected
in a lake but then disturbed by the hermit's doubts, as if a stone
had been thrown in the water, so that "glimmering fragments of a
broken sun, / Banks, trees, and skies in thick disorder run" (A,
100). Here too the sun is an image of cosmic order and disorder,
and it is the disturbance that causes God to send "an angel down
to calm thy mind" (A, 107).

Parnell's poem is therefore evidently in a sense a celebration of
the status quo. The angel's actions really serve to vindicate the
present order in partially correcting it. The hermit is wrong to
question the distribution of wealth: "And why should such, within
himself he cried, / Lock the lost wealth a thousand want beside?"
(A, 104) This is a characteristically eighteenth-century theodicy
(ultimately stoic or Neoplatonic in origin), not the basic biblical
view that there is injustice in the present order, which deeply offends
God, and that He will come to set it right in the end. Parnell's
aspirations toward the sublime in the earlier poetry have turned into
an eighteenth-century celebration of God's order. The bare and
primitive narrative in the sources has become something of elegant
formality, with a touch of fashionable sentiment.

Yet Parnell's movement toward polish does not prevent his Christianity from retaining a certain solidity. He wins Professor Fairchild's approval for not letting the sentiment with which his doctrines
are presented swamp them completely. It is, in fact, his sense of
God's ordered providence that he is most successful in conveying,
not the intimate religious emotion that was obviously real enough
in itself to him. Something of the latter quality survives, however,

into the later work, to blend attractively with the new control. His self-image is not that of a worldly man-about-town like Matthew Prior, but rather of a Christian gentleman like Addison, truly pious, but moderate and polite too, careful to avoid both enthusiasm and too direct a didactic mode. It is clear that Parnell develops toward this approach through mixing in the politest circles.

Some later poems seem to involve no more than a stylish expression of conventional morals. In others like "The Hermit" or "An Allegory on Man" the moral intention is obviously more genuine, and the increase in brevity and control and stylishness certainly helps it to be more effectively expressed. It is the way Parnell manages to retain a certain emotional freshness and Christian sincerity from his earlier writings and yet combine it with a beautifully polished conventionalism, and even with wit and irony, that gives his poetry it characteristic attractiveness. The great improvement in his work, despite an inevitable narrowing of range, can hardly be denied, and it is clear that there were real advantages in the polite mode for a minor poet of genuine talents.

Chapter Seven
Parnell's Prose

No one would consider Parnell a major prose writer, but his prose is of some interest in its relationship to the various currents of the period as well as to his poetry. He was respected for his scholarship, and he wrote brief critical remarks of real interest, several periodical essays, and a satire that was the first Scriblerian piece to be published.

The Prose Allegories

The first piece ever published by Parnell was the prose Vision in *Spectator* no. 460 on 18 August 1712. This was followed by three other published periodical essays. They can be linked with the comments on allegory written about the same time in the Preface to his *Essay on the Different Styles of Poetry*.

Allegory had become a much-discussed topic among critics.[1] Late medieval writers including Dante and Boccaccio had considered moral allegory the central justification for poetry and saw the poet as conveying hidden truths by this means. The stories of classical mythology in particular were read in this way. The growth of rationalism and scientific attitudes altered these views and made neoclassical critics suspicious of extended fictions and of offenses against Aristotelian probability. Their high regard for classical epic made them continue to explain away the fictions found therein as didactic allegories, but they made a distinction between them and the wilder fictions of Spenser.

Defenses of allegory in the late seventeenth century tended to be moralistic and cautious, as in Sir Richard Blackmore's remarks:

There is indeed a way of writing purely Allegorical, as when Vices and Virtues are introduced as Persons, the first as Furies, the other as Divine Persons or Goddesses, which still obtains, and is well enough accommodated to the present Age. For the Allegory is presently discern'd and the Reader is by no means impos'd on, but sees it immediately to be an Allegory and is both delighted and instructed with it.[2]

In Addison's *Tatler* and *Spectator* essays we find considerable interest in allegory. He devotes high praise to it and takes the discussion further than his recent predecessors. We see a growing attraction to allegory not for its didactic but for its picturesque and imaginative qualities and a new sympathy for Spenser. In *Spectator* no. 419 Addison links allegories with what he calls the "Fairy Way of Writing." The same type of imagination required to write about imaginary beings like fairies is also required when the poet "represents any Passion, Appetite, Virtue or Vice, under a visible shape and makes it a person or an Actor in his poem." He says that Milton was the first to write of personified abstractions that were not part of a continuous allegorical narration. This kind of writing is "more difficult than any other that depends on the poet's Fancy because he has no pattern to follow in it, and must work altogether out of his own invention."[3]

In the preface to his *Temple of Fame* Pope justified his choice of an allegorical subject and praised the mode. We may speculate whether he influenced Parnell in this respect or Parnell him. It is known that the writing of the *Temple of Fame* preceded its publication by several years. It is not certain, however, what degree of intimacy had been established between Pope and Parnell before the publication of the latter's *Essay upon the Different Styles of Poetry* in December 1712, though some contact there definitely was. The two works probably reflect independent responses to the interest in allegory in Addison's circle.

Like Pope, Parnell in his brief prefatory remarks to an *Essay upon the Different Styles of Poetry* indicates the ancient origins of allegory and appears at this stage to accept the view that the stories of the heathen gods were all allegorical ways of conveying moral truths. In the preface to his *Iliad,* however, Pope questioned whether modern poets should continue to use allegory.[4] So Parnell does seem to go beyond Pope in echoing Addison's ideas by praising allegory for its originality: "And indeed there seems to be no likelier way by which a poetical genius may yet appear as an original than that he should proceed with a full compass of thought and knowledge either to design his plan or to beautify the parts of it, in an allegorical manner" (C, 412). He goes on to say that if writers exclude their own invention they are in danger of simply being imitators of the classics, "a borrowing from others, which we must agree together not to call stealing, because we take only from the ancients." He praises Spenser and Milton for their invention, "which is not bounded by what has been seen before" (C, 413). Like the poem itself, these remarks are not to be regarded as "romantic" but rather as an illustration of R. S. Crane's point that the system we call neoclassicism held in rich tension such ideas as imitation and originality, judgment and fancy, emphasizing now the one side now the other as occasion demanded rather than being committed in a static way on either side of the balance.[5]

The genre of prose allegories and visions obviously reflects this new interest in allegory in the period. Addison was not the first to introduce prose allegories into periodicals, but, as John Hughes points out in his essay on allegory,[6] he was certainly the real innovator insofar as he popularized the idea and produced many fine examples. These prose allegories descend from popular classical allegories like Prodicus's *Choice of Hercules* and Cebes's *Tablature of Human Life*.[7] Addison's *Tatler* no. 97, for example, is a paraphrase of Prodicus. They also show the influence of Spenser and of the masques of Ben Jonson and James Shirley. They encourage a dignified and generalized statement of moral truths with some imaginative power, and they are, broadly speaking, an aspiration to a rational and didactic version of the baroque sublime.

Parnell's *Spectator* no. 460 begins with the general moral statement that we are often unaware of our own defects and follies or, indeed, are proud of them. The moral teaching is, of course, highly traditional, Socratic, but also particularly a sixteenth-, seventeenth-, and eighteenth-century French theme (Montaigne, La Rochefoucault, Pascal), taken up by Pope ("Man Know thyself") and Arbuthnot (in the poem "Know Thyself"). Parnell gives an account of the Hill where Error and Opinion dwell, from which he sees the Palace of Vanity. The general conception relates to Chaucer's House of Fame and Milton's Paradise of Fools, though it is interesting to see how Parnell has made the details of the architecture contemporary, as with the landscape of "The Hermit": "The walls were gilded all for show; the lowest set of Pillars were of the slight Fine Corinthian Order, and the Top of the Building being rounded, bore so far the Resemblance of a Bubble."[8] The latter touch is a nice one—the fashionable dome is also the fragile bubble of vanity. Within the hall are found Honour, Ostentation, Gallantry, and Self-Conceit. A plain-dealing old man tries to pierce the illusions, but is driven away. Then a crowd of harpies flocks in, and as the inhabitants flee they become aware of the terrible instability of the whole building.[9]

Spectator no. 501, appearing on 4 October 1712, concerns the subject of grief, and has been said, with no more than circumstantial evidence, to be about Parnell's reactions to the death of his wife. Refusing to listen to Patience, the narrator and his companions set out upon the river of tears and come to an island overcast with fogs. At the heart of it is the Grotto of Grief. The description here, derived from Spenser's Cave of Despair, has a certain melodramatic power. Some are overcome in this spot, but others manage to escape, and regain the company of Patience. In telling each other their stories they "mutually gave and received pity, and so by degrees became tolerable company."[10] They experience "Gleams of Amusement" and eventually return to the other shore. Whatever its relationship to Parnell's own life, this is perhaps the most interesting of his visions. The description is well done, and there is some psychological sensitivity. A feeling that mourning is inevitable plays against an Augustan sense that it is wrong to give in to it.

The *Guardian* no. 56 is a dream vision about the difference between Reproof and Reproach. By means of an allegorical landscape Parnell shows that Reproof is the middle way between Reproach and Flattery. This is a subject of central importance to writers in a polite age in which satire was popular. Parnell's discussion links up, for example, with debates about the relative merits of Horace's good-natured satire and Juvenal's outspokenness. Another linked topic of discussion in the period was the difference between gentlemanly "raillery" and impolite "railling." Richard Flecknoe says, for example, that "raillery" "differs from Gybing, as gentle smiles from scornful laughter, and from rayling as Gentlemen playing at Foyls from Butchers and Clowns playing at Cudgels."[11] Parnell's commitment to a more Horatian satire and to "raillery" rather than "railling" is made clear.

The *Guardian* no. 66 deals with the topic of scandal and gossip. Parnell has a vision of a solemnity celebrated at the House of Common Fame by Curiosity, Talkativeness, Censoriousness, and Credulity. The general conception of the allegory is again Chaucer's, and the details are light social satire similar to Pope's in *The Rape of the Lock*. This tone continues with the actual description of the House and an account of the tea-drinking libation as the "Hecatomb of Reputations":

In the middle stood a Table finished after the manner of the remotest
Asiatick countries, upon which the Lamp, the Silver Vessel, and cups of
white Earth, were planted in order. Then dried Herbs were brought,
collected for the Solemnity in Moonshine, and Water being put to them,
there was a greenish liquor made, to which they added the Flower of Milk
and an Extraction from the Canes of America, for performing a Libation
to the infernal Powers of Mischief. [12]

The final vision remained unpublished until the appearance of
Pope's *Poems on Several Occasions by Thomas Parnell*. [13] The narrator is
taken up into the air and comes to a land of strange inhabitants.
The vision is more of a riddle than a moral allegory, for the explanation that these creatures are books is not given until the end. The
general idea seems to come from Swift's *Battle of the Books* and is
carried out rather mechanically. [14]

This final vision is certainly inferior to the other four. All five,
with the possible exception of the essay on bereavement, deal with
topics that are of common interest among the *Spectator* writers and
the Scriblerus group. They have poetic touches and flashes of color,
but their mode seems a very dated one now, and if Parnell had not
become a well-known poet they would not have received any
attention.

"Life of Homer"

The first volume of Pope's long-awaited translation of the *Iliad*
was published in June 1715. Prefixed to it was the lengthy "Essay
on the Life, Writings and Learning of Homer" by Parnell, whose
"good-nature," Pope said in the Preface, "is no less extensive than
his learning." [15] Certainly this essay was far from being the only or
indeed the main contribution Parnell's good nature made to Pope's
Iliad. Though not a professional scholar he was very learned. As
Maynard Mack says, the most striking thing about the essay itself
is its range and accuracy of reference. [16] In approximately sixty pages
Parnell quotes more than fifty authors, none of whom is English,
and most of them more than once from different works. The references are accurate and so, it appears, are the translations and
transcriptions.

Pope's letters make clear how much use he made of Parnell's
learning apart from the essay itself. He writes to Parnell: "You are
a Generous Author, I a Hackney Scribler, You are a Grecian and

bred at a University, I a poor Englishman of my own Educating."
Elsewhere in another previously quoted letter he writes in a passage
where the humor does not detract from the sense of desperation:
"The minute I lost you Eustachius with nine hundred pages, and
nine thousand contractions of the Greek character arose to my view—
Spondamus with all his Auxiliaries in Number a thousand pages
(Value three shillings) and Dacier's three volumes, Barnes' two,
Valterie's three, Cuperus half in Greek, Leo Allatius three parts in
Greek, Scaliger, Macrobius, & (worse than 'em all) Aulus Gallius."[17]
One cynical commentator said that Pope simply versified his *Iliad*
from a prose translation provided by Parnell. This was certainly far
from the case. Pope's own reading in the commentators has been
shown to be extensive. Nevertheless, Parnell's help was invaluable.
He provided digests of the commentators and Mack says that "we
may fairly guess that a large number of the learned extracts for the
earlier annotations came from his friend."[18]

What we would regard as more scientific and scholarly approaches
to Homer were only just beginning at this time with Dr. Bentley
and Thomas Hearne, and they had little influence on either Pope
or Parnell. The neoclassical consensus had been that Homer's work
was of supreme value for the timeless moral truths it contained. To
most critics Homer was a mine of universal knowledge, containing,
as Anthony Collins wrote, the "Principles of all Arts and Sciences,"[19]
and every aspect was allegorical, so that anything that seemed un-
worthy of the poet could be explained away.

The view that Homer's work was essentially timeless had been
disturbed by the Ancients and Moderns controversy, the great cul-
tural debate in France and to a lesser extent in England between
the exponents of the classics and the supporters of the idea of progress
and the new science. The moderns rejected the view that Homer
was a mine of universal knowledge and emphasized that he belonged
to a particular period. Madame Dacier, the authority Pope most
respected, was influenced by these attitudes of the Moderns, but
used them in Homer's defense. Knowledge of Homer's period would
help us to understand him better and to sympathize more with what
might otherwise seem defects.

Parnell's essay is not remarkable for its originality. What Pope
wanted and what Parnell was admirably equipped to provide was a
compendium of received opinion. He begins with an analysis of the
different kinds of stories about Homer that have come down to us.

He reveals a skeptical intelligence. He gives sound semantic reasons for being doubtful about the names in the Homeric genealogies, for example, and he is able to differentiate genuine material from spurious. He does not commit himself on the subject of the authenticity of the *Batrachomuomachia,* ("Battle of the Frogs and Mice") despite his own fondness for it. In his comments on the legends on Homer's birth we see how far the spirit of scholarship, historical accuracy, and enlightenment had come in England since the not-too-distant days of Sir Thomas Browne:

These are the extravagant stories by which Men, who have not been able to express how much they admire him, transcend the Bounds of Probability to say something extraordinary. The mind, that becomes dazled with the Sight of his Performances, loses the Common Idea of a Man in the fancy'd Splendor of Perfection. It sees nothing less than a God worthy to be his Father, nothing less than a Prophetess deserving to be his Nurse, and, growing unwilling that he should be spoken of in a Language beneath its Imaginations, delivers Fables in the place of History.[20]

Parnell next looks at the more probable conjectures about Homer's country and his travels, and discusses what can be found out about the poet from the works themselves. In the second section he discusses the history of the poems and their reputation. In the final section he goes on to describe the state of society in Homeric times under such headings as "poetry," "theology," "politics," and "history." As Donald Foerster says, he is "one of the first to suggest that a complete picture of historical backgrounds, not a picture based on selected facts, is of considerable value to the reader and student of Homer."[21] In this respect he influenced Thomas Blackwell, who elaborated on Parnell and took this approach further in 1735.

Parnell's basic approach is humanist but skeptical, neoclassical but incorporating, like Madame Dacier, some of the new historical insights. It is ridiculous, Parnell feels, to attribute to Homer the purpose of providing an encyclopaedia of all knowledge, yet Homer was a "Father of Learning," and ethical and humane wisdom is diffused throughout his works. We can see, for example, that Homer is a "compassionate Lover of Mankind, from his numberless Praises of Hospitality and Charity." If his poems are "not now receiv'd for a Rule of Life," they are yet more deeply valued "for those just Observations which are dispers'd through them."[22]

Parnell's attitude to allegorical interpretations is similar. Francis Bacon had been skeptical about the hidden meanings in Homer, but Le Bossu and Madame Dacier reaffirmed them. So did English critics like Thomas Rhymer and John Dennis. Even Addison appears to say in places that Homer's gods are all allegorical.[23] Parnell reveals a moderate skepticism within an overall acceptance of the tradition. Homer took his gods as he found them. There is no point in allegorizing everything like those who "tried to carry on everywhere that vein of Allegory which was already broken open, with success in some places." Yet if Parnell opposes oversystematization, he reaffirms that Homer's gods have an allegorical aspect: there are "several Rays of Truth streaming through all this Darkness, in those Sentiments he entertains concerning Providence of the Gods, delivered in several Allegories lightly veil'd over."[24]

The general tone of Parnell's essay is dry. Yet, as Maynard Mack explains, Pope wanted this air of scholarly objectivity here, which "makes an admirable foil to the glowing enthusiasm" of his own preface. Later, however, Pope was to complain: "It is still stiff, and was written stiffer; as it is, I verily believe it cost me more pains in the correcting, than the writing it would have done." He also asked Warburton to revise it for a new edition, saying, "I would willingly render it a little less defective."[25]

Yet there are flashes of enthusiasm and interest here too, as well as the impressive display of learning. Beneath the deliberately dispassionate tone lies a real admiration that is all the more impressive for being combined with demystification: "And even after the Abatement of what was extravagant in his Run of Praise, he remains confessedly a mighty Genius not transcended by any which have since arisen; a Prince, as well as a Father, of Poets."[26]

Scriblerian Writings and *The Life of Zoilus*

During the period in which Parnell helped Pope with the Homer translation he also took part in all the activities of the Scriblerus Club. Pope suggested to Gay late in 1713 that they and a group of their friends work together on a monthly journal that would satirize false learning by means of ironic reviews. The group that eventually gathered included Pope, Swift, Gay, Arbuthnot, Parnell, and occasionally Harley. At the end of the Christmas season it began to meet together as a club. The main business of the meetings was to discuss the project and the drafts brought forward by the members. Something of its sociable spirit has already been described. Goldsmith seems to catch the playful tone when he says of the Scriblerus group in his *Life of Parnell* that it was "a society in which of all others a man might be most foolish without incurring any danger of contempt."[27] Gradually the objects of satire widened to include the whole range of what they regarded as degenerate modern intellectual interests. The group was conservative in politics, and intellectually it espoused the older Renaissance humanist view that learning should be an education for living. The club disliked the new science for what seemed its irrelevance to moral concerns and the new textual criticism of Dr. Richard Bentley for what seemed its distortion of the humane spirit of the text in the interests of pedantic detail.

The proliferation of satiric detail and subject matter necessitated a unifying scheme. This developed with the idea of a biography of Martinus Scriblerus, the pedant-hero. The different stages of his education would provide the opportunity for satire of the different kinds of learning.[28]

In this first period of Scriblerus activity, in the year 1714, the only period in which Parnell was closely involved, the general plan of the work was made and its opening chapters, which tell of Martinus's birth and education, were written, along with chapters on the freethinkers, diseases of the mind, and other brief episodes. Arbuthnot was a distinguished physician and scientist, but Parnell was certainly the best informed of the group in the classics and in ancient philosophy. We have no way of working out exactly what part the different collaborators played. The book as first published in the second volume of Pope's works in 1741 is a composite of ideas and stretches of writing by the various club members. Swift wrote at one point that "Parnell has some ideas of it but is idle."[29] Parnell and Arbuthnot were probably the most likely candidates to have written the chapters on logic and metaphysics and on the freethinkers, though Kerby-Miller believes that Arbuthnot is the more likely of the two.

Chapter 7 consists of a parody of the abuse of logic among classical, medieval, and Renaissance thinkers including Aristotle, St. Thomas Aquinas, and Locke. Though Kerby-Miller does not say so, Parnell as a clergyman must surely be a more likely source than Arbuthnot for chapter 12 on the freethinkers. In it Martin attempts to discover the seat of the soul, which he takes to be in the pineal gland. The Society of Freethinkers at the Grecian Coffeehouse write to him to prove by a mechanical analysis of thought processes that the soul does not exist. The satire here glances at the materialism of Descartes and, in particular, as Robert Steensma shows, at the debate about the materiality of the soul between the freethinker Anthony Collins and the metaphysician Samuel Clarke in the first decade of the century.[30] Still, these concerns are also close to Swift's in "The Mechanical Operation of the Spirit," for example, and all we can be sure of is that Parnell's knowledge and ideas at the very least played a background part in the work of this period.

In 1732 there appeared in the third volume of the *Miscellanies* of Pope and Swift (1732), "An Essay of the Learned Martinus Scriblerus Concerning the Origin of the Sciences, Written to the Most Learned Dr. ———, F. R. S., from the Deserts of Nubia." Pope makes it clear that this was written by Arbuthnot in conjunction with himself and Parnell. Presented through the persona of Martin, its aim is to satirize the methods of argument of those who make assertions on faulty assumptions or based on one or two facts. Martin tries to prove that a race of ancient pygmies was responsible for the origin of learning, since all the ancient races remarkable for learning can be proved by various references to have been in touch with such a people. Needless to say, all the references Martin adduces are ambiguous and misleading ones. It has been suggested that Parnell's main contribution to this essay was to supply these classical references, of which good satiric use is made. Martin argues, for example, that we can tell from their appearances that Aesop and Socrates were descended from these pygmies. The essay concludes by saying that if only we were gentler we could tame their descendants to pass on their learning again, and moves into the Swiftian-sounding vision of the different sorts of men who could be taught by the different species: "The man-tygers to instruct heroes, statesmen and scholars; baboons to teach ceremony and address to courtiers; monkeys, the art of pleasing in conversation, and agreeable affections to ladies and their lovers; apes of less learning, to form comedians and dancing-masters; and marmosets, court pages and young English travellers?"[31]

Closely connected both with the Scriblerus Club and with Pope's Homer is *The Batrachomuomachia with The Life of Zoilus and his Remarks*. This was originally intended to appear with the first volume of the *Iliad*, but is obviously an example of Parnell's well-known dilatoriness. Parnell began its composition during 1714 during the prolonged stay in England and took it back to Ireland to complete it. It was not in fact published until 1717. We have already considered the translation as poetry. Here it is the significance of the work as a whole that concerns us. One thing immediately evident is Pope's eagerness for its publication. Early in 1716 he writes: "If I were to tell you the thing I wish above all things, it is to see you again; the next is to see here your Treatise of Zoilus. . . . I question not the prose is as excellent in its sort as the Essay on Homer: Nothing can be more glorious to that great Author, than that the same hand that carvd his best Statue, and deckd it with its old Lawrells, should also hang up the Scare-crow of his miserable Critick, and gibbet up the Carcase of Zoilus, to the Terror of the Writings of Posterity."[32]

His delighted reaction when the work appeared is equally apparent: "Gay's play, among the rest, has cost much time and long suffering; to stem a tide of malice and party, that certain authors have raised against it, the best revenge upon such fellows, is now in my hands, I mean your *Zoilus,* which really transcends the expectation I had conceived of it." In fact Pope makes clear that he actually urged Parnell to compose the work: "To tell you that your translation of the Batrachomuomachia is an excellent piece is no more than every body now knows, and to say that I like it still the better, and am more in your debt than the rest of the world, because it was done at my desire is no more than you know already."[33]

The preface makes it obvious that the primary purpose of the whole work was to provide a concealed manifesto for Pope's translation. Tickell's rival translation was known to be coming out soon after Pope's. The translation of a minor work supposedly by Homer would provide a microcosm of the larger, a "Homer in a Nut-Shell" which would exemplify the principles of the larger translation, and even as Richard Dircks shows, burlesque it in an affectionate manner.[34] The *Life of Zoilus* would similarly deal with its detractors.

The preface begins with the mention of a translator of Homer who is "of a tall presence and thoughtful countenance." This is both a teasing reference to the diminutive Pope and a complimentary pun on the literal meaning of the Greek word *hypsos* ("sublime"), that is, "lofty," "elevated."[35] The discussion that follows serves to explain and justify all the principles behind Pope's translation, the use of blank verse rather than rhyme, for example. Parnell says that he himself resolved to try, as with Pope's Homer, "what is was to translate in the spirit of a writer," and decided on *The Battle of the Frogs and Mice* (135). He says, again with reference to Pope, that he well knows how hard readers are to please in translations of this kind. Nevertheless, he humorously answers all objections beforehand as follows:

When I am literal, I regard my author's words; when I am not, I translate in his spirit. If I am low, I choose the narrative style; if high, the subject required it. When I am enervate, I give an instance of ancient simplicity; when affected, I show a point of modern delicacy. As for beauties, there never can be found one in me, which was not really intended; and for any faults, they proceeded from too unbounded fancy, or too nice judgement, but by no means from any defect in either of those faculties. (139)

Zoilus of Amphipolis was a rhetorician who flourished about 365–336 B.C.[36] He wrote nine volumes of pettifogging criticism of Homer. Parnell's *Life* of him can be seen in a variety of contexts. It looks back, for example, to Pope's own descriptions of bad critics in the *Essay on Criticism*. Pope had mentioned Zoilus there in a first version.[37] John Dennis, a critic notorious for his bad humor and cantankerousness, had certainly been glanced at too in the *Essay on Criticism*. Dennis had replied in kind, and his most recent attack on Pope appeared only three months before Parnell's work. The fact that Parnell began this work as early as he did means that it was not written as a reply to Dennis, though it was an apt rejoinder when it did appear in the May after Dennis's February attack.

Both the *Life* and the *Remarks* are also to be seen in a Scriblerian context. It was in fact the first Scriblerian work to appear in print, and its satire on the foolish critic is obviously a part of the whole attack on the abuses of modern learning. In this respect Dr. Richard Bentley, the great textual critic, is another victim. It had not been forgotten that Bentley had attacked Swift's patron Sir William Temple in his *Dissertation upon the Epistles of Phalaris* (1697). Bentley had been called "Zoilus" by Temple in 1699 in a pamphlet that appeared as part of the controversy.[38]

Parnell begins his *Life* by explaining that a bad critic is merely an addition to the great poet's fame, "placed before him with the justice of antiquity in its sacrifices, when, because such a beast had offended such a deity, he was brought annually to his altar to be slain upon it" (141). He explains that Zoilus was the disciple of a philosopher famous for an envious attack on Socrates. Envy and ill will were the distinguishing marks of Zoilus's personality. Homer was above all others the object of his envy because he had a universal reputation and universal gifts. Zoilus tried to attack Homer at the Olympic games, but was punished for it. Having made his way to Egypt, he attempts to prove that Homer is a bad poet, but is treated with derision. He offends men of wit, who can be compared ". . . to nothing more than to the bee, a creature winged and lively, fond to rove through the choicest flowers of nature, and blest at home among the sweets of its own composition: not ill-natured, yet quick to revenge on injury; not wearing its sting out of the sheath, yet able to wound more sorely than its appearance would threaten" (154).

This passage is obviously derivative from Swift's *Battle of the Books*. It shows Parnell providing a rationale or justification for Pope's attacks on Dennis, and indicates an identification with the poets who retain a tone of courtly wit and ease: "These were the ways of writing which Zoilus hated, because they were not only read, but retained easily, by reason of their spirit, humour and brevity; and because they not only make the man a jest upon whom they are written, but a further jest if he attempts to answer them gravely" (154–55).

It must be admitted that Parnell's tone in this essay is far from subtle. He shows Zoilus, for example, throwing stones at children and feared as giving the evil eye. The tone is comic hyperbole, but it is not successful. The narrative ends with the story of Zoilus's execution in Smyrna after having insulted Homer in that poet's native city. Before his death he prophesies that the French will continue the quarrel by translating Homer into prose. Yet he also sighs because he foresees that there shall "arise a poet in another nation, able to do Homer justice, and make him known amongst his people to future ages" (161). This reference and the final paragraph of the *Life* make clear again that Parnell is attacking critics as detractors in the context of Pope's work.

In the *Remarks of Zoilus* we see the first example of the Scriblerian technique of mock-notes, to be used so elaborately by Pope in the later editions of the *Dunciad*. Overall, however, like the *Life,* they are not very subtle or amusing. Parnell had tried to make contemporary critics ridiculous by describing an unfortunate predecessor. He does the same now by casting his remarks in a form that burlesques their methods. But his satire succeeds in being at the same time both complicated and obvious. In exemplifying dullness and triviality the *Remarks* do not succeed in transcending them by ironic wit. The true tradition of humane criticism is, however, eloquently described at one point: "Criticism indeed deserves a noble elegy when it is enlarged by such a comprehensive learning as Aristotle and Cicero were masters of; when it adorns its precepts with the consummate exactness of Quintilian, or is exalted into the sublime sentiments of Longinus" (176). Above all, the essay manifests a genuine reverence, transcending personal friendship, for the achievement of Pope, and this is the note on which Parnell ends the *Remarks:* "There is no disgrace in being censured, where there is no credit to be favoured. But, on the contrary, envy gives a testimony of some perfection in another; and one who is attacked by many is like a hero whom his enemies acknowledge for such, when they point all the spears of a battle against him. In short an author who writes for every age, may even erect himself a monument of those stones which envy throws at him" (185).

Chapter Eight
Parnell's Reputation and Influence

George Saintsbury wrote perceptively in 1898 that "It is curious that out of the small bulk of Parnell's poetical work, poetical criticism of the most various times and tastes has been able to pick quite different things to sustain his reputation."[1] Yet Parnell is surely, in F. R. Leavis's words, "a representative period figure."[2] He has the gift of beautifully expressing certain interests of the period that were less central to the work of Pope, though even there their presence must not be underestimated. We should extend our sense of the normal boundaries of what we consider "Augustanism" or "neoclassicism" to include this close friend of Pope and Swift, who wrote attractively about nature and sentiment, rather than heralding Parnell as the precursor of what is new.

Nevertheless, the handful of his best poems were highly influential, and allusions to and borrowings from him abound. The elements he selects and beautifully enshrines were more attractive to his successors than the central impulses of Pope's work. As Reuben Brower has explained, poets of the mid-century found it both easier and more congenial to follow Parnell and James Thomson than the poet of the "Moral Essays" and *The Dunciad*.[3] In so doing, as, for example, in the development of sentimental emphases, they also often altered the significance of what they found.

Parnell in the Earlier Eighteenth Century: Elegance and "Simplicity"

Parnell's great popularity and fame is evidenced everywhere in the eighteenth century. A writer in the *London Magazine* in 1770 says that "Dr. Parnell's reputation as a poet has long been universally established, and his writings are so very well known that it is unnecessary for us to characterise them."[4] A couplet from an "Elegy to an Old Beauty" became almost proverbial: "And all that's madly wild, or oddly gay / We call it only pretty Fanny's way."[5] An amusing indication of how widespread the interest in Parnell was can be found in the story in the *Johnsonian Miscellanies* of Johnson's visit to Mr. Wickins, a "respectable draper in Lichfield":

> He then, with some difficulty squeezed himself into a root-house, when his eye caught the following lines from Parnell:
>
> > "Go search among your idle dreams,
> > Your busy or your vain extremes,
> > And find a life of equal bliss,
> > Or own the next begun in this."
>
> The Doctor, however, not possessing any Silvan ideas, seemed not to admit that heaven could be an Arcadia.[6]

In the first edition of his *Essay on the Genius and Writings of Pope* (1756) Joseph Warton placed Parnell in the third class of poets, "men of wit, of elegant taste and fancy in describing familiar life, though not the higher scenes of poetry," but in the second edition Parnell is promoted, together with Prior and Waller, to the second class, "such as possessed the true poetical genius in a more moderate degree, but who had noble talents for moral, ethical and panegyrical poetry." In this category they join Dryden and Pope himself.[7]

As might be expected, the chorus of praise of Parnell began early in the century among his group of friends, the Scriblerus Club and his Anglo-Irish associates. Swift says that Parnell "outdoes all our poets here a Barrs length," and praises *An Essay on the Different Styles of Poetry,* which he says is "mightily esteemed, but poetry sells ill." George (later Bishop) Berkeley also praises *An Essay on the Different Styles of Poetry.*[8] What is interesting is not so much the fact of this praise of Parnell by Pope, Swift, and their circle, who must be considered interested parties, but what they chose to concentrate on. What Pope really seems to admire is Parnell's classical elegance, and he links the poetic quality with his friend's social gifts, as we have seen, "With softest manners, gentlest arts, adorn'd." Parnell is proficient in a variety of meters, "blest in ev'ry strain," as well as learned, "blest in each science." His classical translations especially impress Pope. He calls the "Vigil of Venus" and *The Battle of the Frogs and Mice* "masterpieces," and says of the latter that he

can "scarce see any thing to be altered in this whole piece." Of the
mass of poems that Parnell sent him he picks out for especial mention
"Hesiod" and "Health: an Eclogue": "The story of Pandora, and
the Eclogue upon health, are two of the most beautiful things I
ever read. I don't say this to the prejudice of the rest, but as I have
read these oftener . . . ."[9]

One of the most influential references to Parnell was David Hume's
in his essay "Of Simplicity and Refinement in Writing."[10] This
relates Parnell to the eighteenth-century fashion for "simplicity,"
described in an important article by R. D. Havens.[11] This simplicity
is far from plainness or a low style as such, though Joseph Spence
did write that Parnell was too low in some places.[12] But the simple
style is actually seen as the apex of polite, controlled art, and it
links up with eighteenth-century classicism and with the idea of
polish and refinement in the sense of refining away false elaboration.

Simplicity is not solely a matter of style, as Hume's remarks make
clear. He agrees with Addison and Johnson that "fine writing consists of sentiments which are natural without being obvious."
Thoughts that are merely natural are too commonplace to engage
us; those that are merely surprising cannot give "any lasting enter-
tainment to the mind." We ought, however, to be more careful of
being over-refined than of being over-simple. Those "compositions
which we read the oftenest, and which every man of taste has got
by heart, have the recommendation of simplicity, and have nothing
surprising in the thought, when divested of that elegance of expression and harmony of numbers, with which it is clothed." Wit pleases
the first time it surprises us, but thereafter we anticipate the thought:
"When I read an epigram of Martial, the first line recalls the whole;
and I have no pleasure in repeating to myself what I know already.
But each line, each word in Catullus, has its merit, and I am never
tired with the perusal of him. It is sufficient to run over Cowley
once; But Parnell after the fiftieth reading is as fresh as the first."[13]

Parnell's simplicity of diction, melodious versification, pleasingly
conventional mature poetry, and gentle emotionalism exercised a
considerable influence on the softer strands of eighteenth-century
poetry. Since this is a matter of general stylistic qualities and the
definitive presentation of what is already conventional, his influence
cannot always be proved where it may be suspected. Several critics
have pointed to such an influence, for example, in the work of
William Collins, Matthew Green, and Thomas Warton the younger.

Collins praised simplicity; his octosyllabic meter may have been influenced by Parnell, and he has a similar lyrical sweetness. In the case of William Shenstone, who has similar stylistic qualities to Parnell, we find in "The Snuff Box" a complimentary reference to the earlier poet, "Immortal Parnell has divinely sung / How from the plastic Hand Pandora sprung."[14] William Hamilton of Bangour and the young John Clare are other examples of poets in the same tradition of lyrical simplicity known to have imitated Parnell directly.[15]

Oliver Goldsmith's interest in Parnell is much more important and clear-cut. His tone and style, with its pure diction, softness of versification, and tenderness approaching to sentimentality are all very close to Parnell, and his direct borrowings are shameless. In the "Threnodia Augustalis," which Goldsmith himself quite accurately called more a "compilation than a poem," there is a direct echo of "A Night Piece on Death," and the whole of "Song, by a Woman" (lines 113–20) is borrowed from "A Hymn to Contentment," an example of imitation or borrowing taken to extremes.[16] Parnell's "Night Piece" was the main influence on Goldsmith's prose essay "A City Night Piece."[17] It is also clear that "The Hermit" influenced "Edwin and Angelina," sometimes called "The Hermit," and put forward by Mr. Burchell in chapter 8 of *The Vicar of Wakefield* as a model of true simplicity.[18]

Parnell in the Later Eighteenth Century: The Poet as Moralist

Johnson's "Life of Parnell" was somewhat overshadowed by Goldsmith's[19] but Johnson has many fascinating references to Parnell elsewhere and in *London* he has a direct borrowing.[20] In the Johnsonian circle a particular interest in Parnell as a moralist is evident. As Donald Davie points out: "The culture of Prior, Lady Mary and Addison differed from that of Goldsmith, Mrs. Boscawen and Johnson chiefly in this—that conversation and letters in the later period are far readier to discuss questions of personal conduct, not under cover of a code of manners, but directly, by appeal to the moral absolutes of Christian tradition."[21] Boswell wrote to Johnson in 1775: "Every scene of my life confirms the truth of what you have told me, there is no certain happiness in this state of being. . . . In your 'Vanity of Human Wishes' and in Parnell's 'Contentment'

I find the only sure means of enjoying happiness, or at least the hope of happiness."[22]

Similarly, Johnson discussed "The Hermit" with great seriousness with a lady who told him that "she has read Parnell's 'Hermit' with dissatisfaction, for she could not help thinking that thieves and murderers who were such immediate ministers from heaven of good to man, did not deserve such punishments as our laws inflict." Johnson replied with an eloquent oration "the substance of which was that because of man's free will he was as deserving of punishment for his evil deeds as if no good had resulted from them."[23]

The separate editions of "The Hermit" that began to appear after about 1750 had a very pious tone. One dated ca. 1760 was called *The Hermit, A Divine Poem; or, A Vindication of Providence;* another, printed in 1774 (price one penny), contains a list of religious tracts "chiefly intended to give away."[24] These show that Parnell was being taken up by the evangelical movement and by the Methodists. Earlier he had appeared in John Wesley's three-volume anthology, *A Collection of Moral and Sacred Poems from the Most Celebrated English Authors.*[25]

If the earnest discussion of Parnell's morality in the Johnsonian circle reflects a similar trend to that of the evangelical movement, Johnson and Goldsmith nevertheless preserve the Horatian emphasis on the combination of pleasure and instruction and even something of the earlier courtly attitude to moral teaching. Johnson himself preferred the racier "Allegory on Man" to the more didactic tone of "The Hermit," and in his Latin epitaph on Parnell he points to the combination of sweetness and piety in the poet's works.[26]

Goldsmith is much more pointed in his condemnation of the "disgusting" solemnity of manner in the poetry of his contemporaries. He praises Parnell's classicism and "simplicity" in his *Life* of the poet and uses the example of his work as a manifesto in favor of the lighter tone and courtly wit of the best early eighteenth-century poetry, "all that agreeable trifling" which "often deceives us into instruction." He says that ". . . it is even virtuous to jest when serious advice might be disgusting. But instead of this, the most trifling performance among us now, assumes all the didactic stiffness of wisdom."[27] This is also the burden of his epitaph on Parnell:

> This tomb inscribed to gentle Parnell's name,
> May speak our gratitude, but not his fame,

What heart but feels his sweetly moral lay,
That leads the truth through pleasure's flowery way?[28]

New Criteria: Sentiment, Originality, Nature Poetry

Though the later period was in some respects more strenuously moralistic than the earlier, it was also much more inclined to mistake emotional excesses for genuine morality, as in some of the "graveyard school" poems and, of course, as the sentimental movement progressed, to indulge in emotionalism purely for its own sake. This was how some nineteenth-century critics made the mistake of talking about Parnell as a preromantic. Certain of his subjects—the hermit, the fairy tale, the graveyard—which were subordinate in his work to his Christian moral concerns, fascinated later poets because of the emotional trappings that they associated with them.

This is certainly the case with "The Hermit," Parnell's most famous poem in the eighteenth and early nineteenth centuries. To this very social age the figure of the hermit exercised a potent fascination, and it soon linked up too with the growing craze for the gothic and the mysteriously medieval. Hermits are ubiquitous in the eighteenth century, found, for example, in David Mallet's "Amyntor and Theodora," in *Rasselas,* in *The Rambler,* no. 65, and in innumerable minor verses. The hermit became a stock figure. Even in the poetry of Wordsworth and Coleridge he can be seen as "a stock poetical recourse not unlike the pseudo-classical devices which they eschewed."[29] Parnell obviously has an important place in this tradition. Though his hermit is still a Christian devotional one rather than a romantic medieval figure, Parnell helped to establish the tradition in its definitive form.

Richard Savage's *The Wanderer* (1729) borrows not only the hermit figure but also some of its leading ideas from Parnell. As with "The Hermit," the poem is a discussion of the problem of evil. The poet has a vision in which he meets a hermit who conducts him to a cell and describes his own past unhappiness. In the last canto there is a transformation scene in which the hermit reveals that he is in fact a seraph, sent to the poet to reveal the true import of all he had seen. The whole scene is very similar to Parnell's conclusion, and there are direct echoes both here and elsewhere in the poem. Savage takes the form as well as the content of his discussion of the problem of evil from Parnell.[31]

Robert Burns continues the conventional interest in the hermit figure in "Despondency" (1786) and also echoes Parnell directly.[32] By the last decade of the century the sentimentalizing of the tradition had gone far, as Samuel Jackson Pratt's "The Hermit and his Dog" shows.[33] It tells the story of a hermit who retires with his faithful dog from the afflictions of life in the world. It is in very bad heroic couplets, but it tries to imitate Parnell's cadences: "In vain the faithful brute was bid to go; / In vain the sorr'wer sought a lonely woe." There is little evidence, however, of Parnell's great theme of the theodicy. Equally, in Parnell's poem there is no equivalent to the sentimentality about the dog and the way it mourns its master, nor of the general sentimentalism of tone, the hermit's "heart that aches if but a wren expire."

In 1793 an anthology entitled *Beauties of the Muses: or, Select Sentimental Poems and Elegies,* which included "The Hermit," was published.[34] The title page announces that these are poems "to wake the soul—to mend the heart." Significant here is the blend of the two meanings of sentimental—these are highly moralistic poems, but the later ones are also contrived to play on the emotions.

With Parnell's "Night Piece" too an emotion that is controlled in the original becomes paramount in some of its successors. It exercised an even greater influence than "The Hermit," though it was probably not so famous. Goldsmith said that it might "with very little amendment be made to surpass all those night pieces and church yard scenes that have since appeared."[35] Here again he was blatantly using Parnell as part of a campaign against the tendencies represented in Thomas Gray's poetry. Johnson did not agree with Goldsmith in this respect at least, differentiating Gray's "Elegy" from his later odes. Guarded support for Goldsmith came, however, from John Young, Professor of Greek at Glasgow, who attacked graveyard poetry for its emotionalism by strict Augustan standards, and said in comparing Gray's and Parnell's poem, "Of the two designs taken in a general view, that of Parnell seems the more perfect."[36]

The vogue for poems on the night and on death in the mid—eighteenth century is remarkable, and Parnell's influence on the mass of minor poetry in the movement is considerable. William

Broome's "Poem on Death" in 1727, is a good example of a close borrowing from Parnell:

> O'er shrouds, and sable falls and mould'ring urns;
> While flowing stables, black plumes and scutcheons spread,
> An idle pomp around the silent dead.

Between 1745 and 1750 several poems called "A Night Piece" were published in the *Gentleman's Magazine*[37] alone.

Parnell also exercised an influence on the major works of the graveyard school. Robert Blair's influential *The Grave* borrows its entire structure from Parnell's poem. There is an early reference to the sickly taper (l. 16), then to the church itself (l. 28), then to the different classes of graves. This description is followed in Blair, as in Parnell, by the apparent rising of spectres. Both poems then move toward the emphasis on resurrection at the close. Verbal reminiscences occur throughout, and Blair's final lines are a direct imitation of the end of "A Night Piece."[38] Yet the effect of Blair's blank verse, with its expansive length and extravagance of tone, is entirely different from Parnell's beautifully neat poem.

James Hervey quotes "A Night Piece" once in the notes to his *Meditations Among the Tombs,* and W. Thomas includes Parnell in the list of sources of Edward Young's *Night Thoughts.*[39] In Blair and in these other two writers we are conscious of the justice of Charles Peake's remark that in the middle and later eighteenth century there was a growing taste for an "emotionally tinged religious attitudinising."[40] Where the "memento mori" aspect of Christian tradition about death grows apart from the other aspects of faith and hope and consolation, then it must be said to have become morbid and to have lost its moorings in revelation. This will still be true if the overall emotional coloring of the work is melodramatic, shivery, gloomy, even if the framework or conclusion is perfectly orthodox consolation. Such a development occurred in the fifteenth century, as Huizinga shows in a famous chapter of *The Waning of the Middle Ages.*[41] It also occurs in the work of Parnell's successors, Blair, Hervey, and Young, though all have perfectly genuine Christian purposes too. Parnell's brevity and control of structure and the symbolic movement from darkness to light means that it is the Christian consolation element that quite properly receives the deepest emphasis. Parnell's successors take up subordinate elements in his work. These elements modulate into sentimental, "graveyard," Gothic, or romantic ideas. Parnell's own beautiful phrasing of these elements is almost definitive, but he is not responsible, of course, for the way that later developments in some respects transform or even reverse his intentions.

Gray's "Elegy in a Country Churchyard" is remarkable among other things for its almost complete lack of Christian feeling or consolation. It seeks rather to explore what could be considered sentimental reflections on the subject of the rural dead. It is obvious that Parnell did influence the poem, though Gray's only recorded reference to Parnell was a contemptuous comment on the *Posthumous Poems*.[42] The general theme of Gray's poem has a close connection with Parnell's idea in "men half-ambitious, all unknown" (A, 94), and a verbal echo has also been noted.[43]

In an interesting comparison Donald Davie has differentiated Gray's sentimentalism from the purity of diction and relatively prosaic soberness of Parnell. Gray writes, for example:

> Full many a gem of purest ray serene
> The dark, unfathomed caves of ocean bear;
> Full many a flower is born to blush unseen
> And waste its sweetness on the desert air.

Agreeing with William Empson, Davie points out that this sentimentalizes and beautifies the lot of the rural poor, suggesting in a sense that they are better off without opportunities. He goes on in a fine piece of analysis to show that Parnell's line "Men half-ambitious all unknown" avoids this "treacherous ambiguity": "If the line read unambitious, the way would be clear: 'Unworried by worldly competition, these men were happy.' Or if read 'all ambitious,' it would spark another ready response: 'men in this humble sphere are worldly as we are, and we, like them, shall be unknown.' Gray, while purporting to say the second, really says the first. Parnell's prosaic 'half-ambitious' says neither, and his pathos is free of any trickery."[44]

Parnell's "Hymn to Contentment" is even less of an actual literary innovation than "A Night Piece." Yet his pleasantly sincere-sounding expression of literary and religious commonplaces made this poem influential too, and its cadences are heard in various minor poems throughout the century.[45] As we have also seen, his "Fairy

Tale" is an early example of the interest in Addison's "fairy way of writing" and in ballad material, and it obviously helped to popularize both.

In Richard Savage and Robert Blair we find poets taking up hints from Parnell and even indeed the key to whole structures and yet altering Parnell's tone completely. The touches of gentle emotionalism in Parnell are always subordinated to Christian doctrine. His "Hermit," for example, is about God's providence, not the romantic attractions of being a hermit. The shift of emphasis in these later poets lends credence to H. N. Fairchild's view that sentimentalism results partly from a liberal Christianity increasingly divorced from actual doctrine.[46] We also see a growing interest in fiction and legends for their own sake as the century progresses, so that there is no longer any emphasis on detached skepticism in works analogous to "A Fairy Tale."

Parnell's "Hermit" and more especially "A Night Piece" were also influential on the Continent. The former was translated by the German poet Johann Bodmer,[47] and the latter by the abbé Yart.[48] "A Night Piece" is also said to have been a precursor of the Italian poet Foscolo's famous *I Sepolcri* ("the tombs").[49]

Several eighteenth- and early nineteenth-century critics praised Parnell's nature poetry. Even Dr. Johnson, in a passage often cited to show that he did have an appreciation of nature, talks of Hawkstone as "a region abounding with striking scenes and terrific grandeur. . . . The ideas which it forces upon the mind are the sublime, the dreadful and the vast. . . . Ilam has grandeur tempered with softness. . . . Hawkstone should be described by Milton, and Ilam by Parnell."[50] But Hugh Blair and William Barron saw Parnell as one of the great original descriptive poets. In *A Synopsis of Lectures on Belles Lettres and Logic* Barron summarizes "descriptive poetry" as follows: "Intended chiefly to gratify the imagination—Appears sometimes in entire poems; but is generally interwoven with other kinds of poetry, particularly Epic and Pastoral. Few original descriptive poets—Thomson, Milton, Parnel, Ossian."[51]

Parnell is surely in strange company here. Hugh Blair makes it easier to understand this. He makes clear that "descriptive Poetry" does not refer only to nature poetry but to the whole rhetorical tradition of "Descriptio," especially discussed in the context of the epic by Le Bossu, which involves any particularized description of objects: "Mr. Parnel's Tale of the Hermit is conspicuous, throughout

the whole of it, for beautiful descriptive Narration. The manner of
the Hermit's setting forth to visit the world; his meeting with a
companion, and the houses in which they are successively entertained
. . . are pieces of very fine painting, touched with a light and
delicate pencil, overcharged with no superfluous colouring, and
conveying to us a lively idea of the objects."[52] In fact, Blair is by
no means revolutionary in his literary theory. Though he stresses
particularity in this lecture 40, so had Lord Kames in his *Elements
of Criticism* in 1762, and Blair is careful to say that the poet should
always mix in human beings with his descriptions of "inanimate
natural objects in order to enliven his description."

Nevertheless, the distinction between Blair's formulation and
Goldsmith's in his *Life of Parnell* is striking. Goldsmith says that
Parnell, "a studious and correct observer of antiquity, set himself
to consider nature with the lights it lent him, and he found the
more aid he borrowed from the one, the more delightfully he re-
sembled the other." Blair writes that "Description is the great test
of a poet's imagination, and always distinguishes an original from
a second rate genius," for where the latter attempts to describe
nature "it appears exhausted by those who have gone before him in
the same tract." He then proceeds to give Parnell as one of his main
examples of the original descriptive poet.[53] Barron's other examples
make it clear that for him more than for Blair nature poetry as such
is the center of interest. So-called "neoclassicism" is a complex
system, but the aspect of originality is undoubtedly receiving greater
emphasis here. Parnell is being considered in the light of similar
criteria to those put forward in Edward Young's *Conjectures on Original Composition* and Joseph Warton's *Essay on Pope*.

Late Augustan versus Early Romantic Views

Older attitudes to Parnell persisted well into the nineteenth century, providing evidence for Leslie Stephen's claim that "the eighteenth century lasted in the upper currents of opinion till at least
1822."[54] In *Readings on Poetry* by R. L. and Maria Edgeworth in
1816 we find an analysis of "Hesiod" that praises its melodious
versification, its classicism, its design, its exactness, and its pleasing
nature imagery.[55] Maria Edgeworth and her father were "late Au-
gustans" rather than romantics in their tastes. Much the same can
be said of the poet Thomas Campbell, who provides one of the most

eloquent appreciations of Parnell's "purity of diction," pinpointing the paradox behind it: "The 'Curiosa Felicitas,' the studied happiness of diction, does not spoil its simplicity. His poetry is like a flower that has been trained and planted by the skill of the gardener, but which preserves in its cultured state the natural fragrance of its wilder air."[56]

The curious late eighteenth-century attempt to read Parnell as a great nature poet was only found among a few critics. Its obverse side was that those who accepted the same criteria about what poetry should be like, yet did not detect such qualities in Parnell, included him in the general dismissal of early eighteenth-century poetry. Thomas Campbell himself obviously feels on the defensive, saying that "There are exclusionists in taste who think that they cannot speak with sufficient disparagement of the English poets of the first part of the eighteenth century. . . . But in poetry 'there are many mansions.' I am free to confess that I can pass from the elder writers and still find a charm in the correct and equable sweetness of Parnell."[57]

The leading romantic poets themselves paid Parnell little attention. Wordsworth made an exception for Lady Winchelsea but not for Parnell in his claim that the poetry of the period intervening from the publication of *Paradise Lost* and *The Seasons* did not contain a single new image of external nature.[58] Coleridge made no reference to Parnell in his criticism, though he copied out the first stanza of "When thy Beauty Appears" as one of his metrical experiments.[59]

The latter poem was also praised by Leigh Hunt in comments that are an amusing mixture of romanticism and Regency gallantry and prurience:

There is a good deal of what the French call 'movement' in the song, besides more passion and colour than are usually to be found in ballads. The heroine looks as if she came upon us fresh from the bath, with all her silks and tresses about her, and the rosy triumph in her face. In the first verse we see nothing but the triumph; in the second we have leisure to consider the woman, and a charming woman she is; in the third, but our criticism will be growing too minute.[60]

In *The Album*, 1822, appeared an essay based on romantic preconceptions that attacks the whole Augustan age for its lack of poetic genius:

In the review of the principal writers of the reign of Anne, what appears chiefly striking to us is the decided lack of genius which it presents. We do not know that there is any period of English literary history at which this want was so great. . . . Parnell wrote but very little and that little does not appear to us of a merit sufficient to entitle him to the fame he acquired. We must conclude that he was one of those persons, who, living much in literary society, and contributing himself, largely to its pleasures, are so frequently and so laudingly mentioned by their more celebrated friends, that they are towed by them, as it were, into fame, with little or no exertion of their own. This applies, though in a far less degree, to Steele. . . . [61]

William Hazlitt had a subtler appreciation of Augustan poetry than the reviewer in *The Album,* but he shared the basic view that it was of an inferior kind. In his *Select British Poets* (1824) he damned Parnell with faint praise, "The praise of Parnell's poetry is, that it was moral, amiable, with a tendency towards the pensive, and it was his fortune to be the friend of poets." In 1818 he had been more open in saying that Parnell was "little more than an occasional versifier." In 1825 he is even ruder: Charles Lamb's taste in books, he says, is fine, and none the worse for being idiosyncratic: "His admiration of Shakespeare and Milton does not make him despise Pope; and he can read Parnell with patience and Gay with delight."[62]

The poet, critic, and bibliographer, Sir Samuel Egerton Brydges, reflects many of the tastes and tendencies of the romantic period. He disliked most eighteenth-century poetry, and he too found Parnell too light-weight: "There is seldom any enthusiasm in the French school of poetry, on which the schools of Dryden and Pope were founded. The best poetry of Queen Anne's reign is flat, and wants vigour and excellence. . . . Parnell is natural, easy and elegant: but he is deficient in terseness and strength; and perhaps in originality . . . ."[63]

Parnell's Later Reputation

By the 1830s Parnell's work was being read less. He retained his status as one of the standard English poets, but only a tiny handful of his poems were widely read and known.[64] Gradually this narrowed itself down to "The Hermit." In 1839 a commentator says that Parnell "was a learned divine and ingenious poet; his moral tale of The Hermit is still held in estimation."[65]

Even of this latter poem, however, a critic wrote in 1837: "The fame of Parnell rests on the Hermit, one of the most beautiful poems in our language [but this] though not forgotten is less read than formerly."[66] Increasingly it was used in Sunday schools and as a text in examinations,[67] but it was less read as a poem in its own right. As the century progressed, Parnell's poetry fell into relative neglect. In 1882 a writer in the *Quarterly Review* said that: "Few things in literary history are more remarkable than the fate which has befallen this once popular poet. . . . His fame has been rapidly declining, and is now almost extinct. We are by no means inclined to set unique value on the poetry of that age, but in our opinion modern criticism has treated Parnell with conspicuous injustice."[68] The dismissal of the Augustan age by critics with romantic preconceptions became a commonplace in later Victorian England, as is shown by the ease with which Matthew Arnold's opinion of Dryden and Pope was allowed to pass. The attitude was crassly displayed by E. K. Chambers in comments on Parnell he wrote in 1894: "He was mediocre even in an age of mediocrity. . . . He had not the keenness of with to grapple successfully with the heroic couplet. . . . The gods had denied him the gift of humour with that of inspiration."[69] W. B. Yeats said in 1895 that Parnell, Denham and Roscommon "were poets but to their own times."[70]

Even Chambers, however, gave tempered praise to "A Hymn to Contentment," and the other side of the Victorian canonization of romantic attitudes was that where Parnell was praised, it was entirely as a preromantic figure. Edmund Gosse, George Saintsbury, Myra Reynolds, and others concentrated attention on the "originality" of his nature poetry and his imaginative qualities, and the "Hymn to Contentment" and "A Night Piece" received more praise than "The Hermit."[71] In 1880, however, Gosse gave outstanding praise to the latter poem, which he said might be "considered as forming the apex and *chef-d'oeuvre* of Augustan poetry in English." It was indeed eccentric at this period to rate Parnell so highly. But Gosse was still a Victorian in his preconceptions, for he said that "A Night Piece" and "A Hymn to Contentment" "possess more real inspiration." In 1889 he wrote: "It would be easy to sustain the thesis that there is more of imagination, in the purely Wordsworthian sense, more of mystery and spirituality, in Parnell than in any other poet of the time."[72] The effect of this was seen in the remarks on Parnell in *All the Year Round* in 1892. This referred to "The Hermit," which "Mr. Edmund Gosse admires so much," and the "Night Piece" and "Hymn to Contentment," "which everybody admires."[73] Partly because of the survival or romantic criteria and partly because of the rise of literary scholarship, Parnell's "Night Piece" has undoubtedly been his best-known poem this century. It has been seen as his most preromantic work and its importance in literary history as a precursor of Blair and Gray has been recognized. Overall, however, the great improvement in the critical stock of eighteenth-century literature has meant the decline of the theory of Parnell as a romantic precursor, but has not led to his sharing in the increased respect accorded to the major figures of the time. Few articles about him and only two editions of his poetry, neither of them of any critical importance, have appeared. The introduction to the first, a generous selection by Hugh de l'Anson Fausset, still saw Parnell in preromantic terms.[74] The main bias of the second, a small selection published by the Cuala Press, Dublin, and edited by Lennox Robinson, was clearly an interest in Parnell as an Irishman.[75]

A. H. Cruikshank wrote a tentative plea for the poet in 1921, "Yet to return to Parnell, I venture to claim that he deserves to be read again."[76] There was also an article on Parnell in the *Dublin Magazine* in 1945, but this virtually dismisses all his work except the "Night Piece," to which it accords extravagant praise, describing it as "a great poem, and we use the word 'great' with a full consciousness of what it means."[77]

H. N. Fairchild's brief account of Parnell in *Religious Trends in English Poetry* is valuable in pointing out that Parnell is a Christian writer rather than a sentimentalist of the later kind or a preromantic.[78] Both James Sutherland and Bonamy Dobrée have helpful comments on the way Parnell tries to relate his poetry to the experiences he has in common with his readers.[79] Donald Davie's *Purity of Diction in English Verse,* published in 1952, refers only briefly to Parnell, but it helps to elucidate the whole context of the poet's work. Davie analyzes Parnell's tone appreciatively and provides in the concept of "purity of diction" a more modern way of looking at what eighteenth-century critics called "simplicity." Without overrating Parnell or seeing him as a precursor of Wordsworth he has put the emphasis on real poetic qualities. In drawing attention in particular to the effect of a "valuable urbanity, a civilized moderation and elegance"[80] he is, of course, stressing exactly that link between social life and literature that was so important to the best writers of the period and that lies behind Pope's praise of Parnell as one "with softest manners, gentlest Arts adorn'd."

Chapter Nine
Conclusion

Thomas Parnell was a distinguished man of letters of his time, with close contacts among all the major figures. His work has a richly representative quality. Even pieces like "A Fairy Tale in the Ancient English Style" or "The Hermit," which seem more unusual, are responses to hints in the greatest compendium of the period's received ideas, the *Spectator*. To see Parnell as some critics have done as a great literary innovator is to misconceive his significance.

Nevertheless, the conventionalism of his poetry has at its best an inspired quality. When we realize that poems like "A Night Piece" are not startling innovations, we are still left to admire Parnell's success in blending the different elements together to create a beautifully finished whole and the way that he gives all his best work a certain stamp of his own. His poetry was of considerable influence, even if his imitators often altered his intentions. His work is deeply informative about the tides of taste in his period. In its classic purity of diction, wit, and stylish conventionalism, it attractively epitomizes the qualities of early eighteenth-century polite verse. What has especially fascinated some readers is the way that this polished tone combines with an apparently artless personal emotionalism, traces of seventeenth-century lyricism, and a Christian sentiment that, although very much of its period, is obviously authentic.

Notes and References

Chapter One

1. *The Poems of Alexander Pope,* ed. John Butt (London: Methuen, 1965), p. 313.
2. For references to these critics see chapter 8.
3. James Miller *Of Politeness* (London, 1738), lines 3–4.
4. Sir Richard Steele, *Spectator,* no. 314, ed. Donald F. Bond (Oxford: Clarendon Press, 1965), 3:138.
5. The best account of the life is P. S. Schoedinger's unpublished Ph.D. thesis, "The Life and Works of Thomas Parnell" (Yale, 1940). Mabel Martin's B.Litt. thesis of the same title (Oxford, 1930) is also useful. There is a memoir by George Aitken in *The Poetical Works of Thomas Parnell* (London, 1894). The quoted phrase is Rev. John Mitford, *The Poetical Works of Thomas Parnell* (London, 1833), p. 3.
6. Schoedinger prints the poem in the appendix to his thesis.
7. Schoedinger, "Life and Works of Parnell," p. 23.
8. Letter of 25 April 1702, in Schoedinger, "Life and Works of Parnell," p. 24.
9. 1705–6, cited in Aitken, *Poetical Works of Parnell,* p. xii.
10. Jonathan Swift, *Journal to Stella,* ed. Harold Williams, 2 vols. (Oxford: Clarendon Press, 1947), 11 August 1711, 1 July 1712, 15 February 1713, pp. 341, 543, 623.
11. *Tatler,* no. 5; *Guardian,* no. 21; *The Tatler and the Guardian Complete in One Volume* (Edinburgh: Nimmo, 1880), pp. 10, 32.
12. Dedication, *Familiar Letters of Love, Gallantry and several occasions by the Wits of the last and present Age* (London: S. Briscoe, 1718).
13. Swift, *Stella,* 18 December 1712, 1 February 1712 [-3], pp. 586, 588, 612.
14. Swift, *Stella,* 27 March 1712 [-3], p. 646; George A. Aitken, *The Life of Steele* (London: W. Isbester, 1889), 1:371.
15. *The Correspondence of Alexander Pope,* ed. George Sherburn (Oxford: Clarendon Press, 1956), 1:195; subsequent citations are to this edition.
16. *The Poems of Jonathan Swift,* ed. Harold Williams (Oxford: Clarendon Press, 1956), 1:188.
17. Pope, *Correspondence,* 2:98.
18. Mitford, *Poetical Works of Parnell,* pp. 56, 57; *Collected Works of Goldsmith,* ed. Arthur Friedman (Oxford: Clarendon Press, 1966), 2:421; hereafter cited as Goldsmith, *Works.*

19. Charles Kerby-Miller, *Memoirs of the Extraordinary Life, Works and Discoveries of Martinus Scriblerus* (New York: Russell & Russell, 1966), p. 41.

20. *The Correspondence of Jonathan Swift,* ed. Harold Williams (Oxford: Clarendon Press, 1963), 2:46; Pope, *Correspondence,* 2 September 1714, 1:249.

21. Pope, *Correspondence,* 25 May or 1 June 1714, 1:225–26.

22. Pope, *The Iliad of Homer,* Books X-XXV, ed. Maynard Mack, in the Twickenham Edition of *The Poems of Alexander Pope* (New Haven: Yale University Press, 1967), 7:578.

23. Aitken, *Poetical Works of Parnell,* p. xxx.

24. "To Mr. Pope," *Poetical Works of Parnell,* ed. Aitken, p. 70. This is the only critical edition yet available; hereafter cited in the text as A, followed by page number. The poems Aitken omits are quoted from *The Works of the English Poets,* vol. 9, ed. Alexander Chalmers (London, 1810); hereafter cited in the text as C, followed by page number. A definitive edition is in preparation by C. J. Rawson and F. P. Lock.

25. Owen Ruffhead, *Life of Alexander Pope* (London: C. Bathurst, 1769), p. 492.

26. Pope, *Correspondence,* 2 September 1714, 1:249.

27. Kerby-Miller, *Scriblerus,* p. 358.

28. Pope, *Correspondence,* 12 December 1718, 1:24.

29. Goldsmith, *Works* 3:409.

30. Pope, *Correspondence,* 29 July 1716; 25 May or 1 June 1714, 1:348, 225.

31. Bath, 4 May 1717, Martin, "Life and Works of Parnell," p. xliii.

32. Swift, *Stella,* 1 March 1712 [-3], p. 642; Pope, *Correspondence,* 29 July 1716, 1:348.

33. *Reliquiae Hearnianae,* 26 May 1734, ed. Philip Bliss (London: Smith, 1869), 3:139.

34. James Boswell, *Life of Johnson,* ed. G. Birkbeck Hill, revised L. F. Powell (Oxford: Clarendon Press, 1934–50), 3:155; 4:398; hereafter cited as Boswell's *Johnson.*

Chapter Two

1. Pope, *Correspondence,* 12 December 1718, 2:24. Joseph Spence, *Observations, Anecdotes and Characters of Books and Men,* ed. James Osborn (Oxford: Clarendon Press, 1966), no. 139, 1:58.

2. Schoedinger, "Life and Works of Parnell."

3. *The Critical Review,* August 1758, p. 121; *Lives of the Poets,* ed. G. Birkbeck Hill (Oxford: Clarendon Press, 1905), 2:54.

4. C. J. Rawson, "Swift's Certificate to Parnell's Posthumous Works," *Modern Language Review* 57 (1962):179–82.

5. Du Bartas's poem was published in 1574. Joshua Sylvester's translation appeared in 1605.

6. Isaac Watts, Preface to *Horae Lyricae*, 8th ed. (London: J. Bradstone, 1743), p. xxi.

7. Longinus was translated in 1674. The most relevant study of the whole topic is David B. Morris, *The Religious Sublime: Christian Poetry and Critical Tradition in Eighteenth Century England* (Kentucky: University Press, 1972).

8. Maren-Sofie Rostvig, *The Happy Man* 2 vols. (Oslo: University Press, 1954, 1958), vol. 2, chap. 4.

9. See, for example, George Williamson, "The Restoration Revolt against Enthusiasm," *Seventeenth Century Contexts* (Chicago: University Press, 1961), pp. 202–39.

10. Sir Philip Sidney, "An Apologie for Poetry," *Elizabethan Critical Essays*, ed. G. G. Smith (Oxford: Clarendon Press, 1904), 1:158.

11. Abraham Cowley, *Poems*, ed. A. R. Waller (Cambridge: University Press, 1905), p. 183.

12. Accounts of poems on this theme can be found in Rostvig, *The Happy Man* 1:210, 304–308; 2, chap. 4; and H. N. Fairchild, *Religious Trends in English Poetry* (New York, 1939), 1:109, 144, 184.

13. "The Dream," Fairchild, *Religious Trends* 1:143.

14. Cited in Morris, *Religious Sublime*, p. 105.

15. Charles Peake, *Poetry of the Landscape and the Night*, (London: Edward Arnold, 1967), p. 82.

16. Fairchild, *Religious Trends*, 1:234; H. Grant Sampson, *The Anglican Tradition in Eighteenth-Century Verse* (The Hague: Mouton, 1971), p. 149.

17. Evelyn Underhill, *Worship* (London: Nisbet, 1936), p. 175, cited Sampson, p. 150.

18. Sampson, *Anglican Tradition*, p. 134.

Chapter Three

1. John Donne, *The Satires, Epigrams and Verse Letters*, ed. W. Milgate (Oxford: Clarendon Press, 1967), lines 11–15, p. 11.

2. Donald Davie, *Purity of Diction in English Verse* (New York: Oxford University Press, 1953).

3. "A Discourse on Pastoral Poetry," *Literary Criticism of Alexander Pope*, ed. Bertrand A. Goldgar (Lincoln, Nebr.:University Press, 1965), p. 93.

4. Swift, *Correspondence*, 26 March 1722, 2:424. There was in fact no separate Dublin edition at this time.

5. Aitken, p. 169; Pope, *Essay on Criticism,* in *Poems,* line 357, p. 74.

6. R. S. Crane, "On Writing the History of Criticism in England, 1650–1800," *The Idea of the Humanities and other Essays* (Chicago: University Press, 1967), pp. 157–75. There is a helpful edition of Parnell's poem in *Different Styles of Poetry,* ed. Robert Mahoney, Irish Writings from the Age of Swift (Dublin: Cadenus Press, 1978.)

7. See C. J. Rawson, "New Parnell Manuscripts," *Scriblerian* 1 (Spring, 1969):1–2. Through the kindness of Professor Rawson and F. P. Lock, who are preparing the edition, I have been able to consult this material.

Chapter Four

1. Ambrose Philips, *The Free Thinker,* no. 124, 29 May 1719.

2. J. W. Saunders, "The Stigma of Print," *Essays in Criticism* 1(1959):139–64.

3. Goldsmith, *Works* 3:407.

4. Pope, "Epistle to Dr. Arbuthnot," in *Poems,* 1. 44, p. 599.

5. In the Preface to Pope's 1717 volume, for example.

6. Jonathan Swift, "Polite Conversation," *Proposal for Correcting the English Tongue: Works,* ed. Herbert Davis (Oxford: Basil Blackwell, 1959), pp. 116–17.

7. Bertrand Bronson, "The Writer," *Man Versus Society in Eighteenth Century Britain,* ed. James Clifford, (Cambridge: University Press, 1968), pp. 108–9.

8. W. H. Auden, comp., *The Oxford Book of Light Verse* (Oxford: University Press, 1938), p. xii.

9. R. D. Havens, "Changing Taste in the Eighteenth Century," *Publications of the Modern Language Association* 44 (1929):501–36.

10. For these and other references see R. Kraft, "Class Analysis of a Literary Controversy: Wit and Sense in Seventeenth Century English Literature," *Science and Society* 10(1946):80–92.

11. E. N. Hooker, "Pope on Wit: The *Essay on Criticism,*" in *Eighteenth-Century English Literature: Modern Essays in Criticism,* ed. James Clifford (New York: Oxford University Press, 1959), pp. 42–61.

12. Daniel Javitch, *Poetry and Courtliness in Renaissance England* (Princeton: University Press, 1978).

13. Pope, "Couplets on Wit," in *Poems,* p. 295.

14. Austin Warren, "Alexander Pope," *Rage for Order: Essays in Criticism* (Chicago: University Press, 1948), chap. 3.

15. Earl of Roscommon, "Essay on Translated Verse," *Criticial Essays of the Seventeenth Century,* ed. J. E. Spingarn, 3 vols., (1908–9; reprint, Bloomington, Ind.: University Press, 1957), 2:306.

16. Jean Le Clerc, 1699; cited by Basil Willey, *The Eighteenth Century Background* (1940; reprint, London: Penguin Books, 1965), p. 31.

17. On this topic see the important study by Jean H. Hagstrum, *Sex and Sensibility: Ideal and Erotic Love from Milton to Mozart* (Chicago: University Press, 1980).

18. See *The Honest Muse* by Rachet Trickett, (Oxford: Clarendon Press, 1967).

19. Chalmers, *Works of the English Poets* 8:403.

20. This is a matter of diction and of phrasing, in the love poetry particularly. Parnell's "Cease, beauty, cease to vex a tender love" ("The Flies," Aitken, p. 78), for example, echoes Granville's "Cease, lover, cease, thy tender heart to vex" (Chalmers, 11:26).

21. James Sutherland, *A Preface to Eighteenth Century Poetry* (1948; reprint, Oxford: University Press, 1962), p. 77.

22. See, for example, John Oldmixon, Preface to *Poems on Several Occasions,* (London, 1696).

23. Lawrence Stone, *The Family, Sex and Marriage in England, 1500–1800* (London: Weidenfeld & Nicolson, 1977).

24. Martin, "Life and Works of Parnell," pp. 57–58. Augurellus wrote in the early sixteenth century.

25. Parnell's source is either the "Legend of Knock Grafton" or a similar Breton legend, as pointed out by Thomas Keightley, *Notes and Queries,* 2d ser., 10 (1860):141.

26. John Dryden, "Dedication to *King Arthur* (1691); Addison, *Spectator,* no. 419, and on ballads, nos. 70, 74.

27. *Catullus, Tibullus and Pervigilium Veneris,* ed. F.W. Cornish, J. P. Postgate, J. W. Mackail, Loeb Classical Library (Cambridge, Mass.: Harvard University Press, 1962), p. 344.

28. Ibid., p. 353.

29. Wayland Hilton-Young, "Translations of the 'Pervigilium Veneris' into English Verse," *Cambridge Journal* 5, no. 6 (March 1952):345.

30. Richard Dircks, "Parnell's 'Batrachomuomachia' and the Homer Translation Controversy," *Notes and Queries* 201 (1956):339–42.

31. R. P. Bond's general study, *English Burlesque Poetry* (Cambridge, Mass.: Harvard University Press, 1932), has a brief account of both Parnell's and Parker's poems.

32. *Athenaeus, The Deipnosophists* 7, trans. Charles Gulick, Loeb Classical Library (Cambridge, Mass.: Harvard University Press, 1939), p. 273; Marion K. Bragg, *The Formal Eclogue in England,* University of Maine Studies, 2d ser. no. 6 (Maine University Press, 1926), pp. 43–44.

33. *Notes and Queries,* 2d ser., 10 (1860):141.

34. Geoffrey Tillotson, "Pope's Epistle to Harley: Analysis," *Pope and his Contemporaries,* ed. James L. Clifford and Louis A. Landa (Oxford: Clarendon Press, 1949), p. 69.

35. Samuel Johnson, *Lives of the English Poets* ed. G. B. Hill (Oxford: Clarendon Press, 1905), 1:467.

36. E. R. Wasserman, "Coleridge's Metrical Experiments," *Modern Language Notes* 55 (1940):432–33.

37. See, for example, *Thraliana,* ed. K. Balderston (Oxford: Clarendon Press, 1951), 2:758.

38. For example, Robert Heron [John Pinkerton], *Letters of Literature* (London, 1785), p. 63.

39. *Works in Verse and Prose: Enlarged with Variations* (Glasgow, 1755).

40. Rawson, "New Parnell Manuscripts," *Scriblerian* 1 (1969):1–2.

41. For a brief study of Pope's revisions in "The Hermit" see A. H. Cruickshank, "Thomas Parnell; or, What was Wrong with the Eighteenth Century?" *Essays and Studies* 7 (1921):65–66.

Chapter Five

1. David Hume, "Of Simplicity and Refinement in Writing," *Essays Moral, Political and Literary,* ed. T. Green and T. Grose, vol. 1 (London: Longmans, 1898); Davie, *Purity of Diction in English Verse* (New York, 1953).

2. Davie, *Purity,* pp. 5, 26, 27.

3. Goldsmith, *Works,* 3:423.

4. Davie, *Purity,* p. 139.

5. See on this topic Clive Probyn, "Realism and Raillery: Augustan Conversation and the Poetry of Swift," *Durham University Journal* 39 (1977):1–14.

6. Havens, "Changing Taste in the Eighteenth Century," *PMLA* 44 (1929).

7. Goldsmith, *Works* 3:422.

8. Ibid., p. 423.

9. Hume, "Of Simplicity and Refinement in Writing," *Essays,* p. 240.

10. Roger Savage, "Swift's Fallen City," *The World of Jonathan Swift,* ed. Brian Vickers (Oxford: Basil Blackwell, 1968), pp. 171–74.

11. John Milton, *Paradise Lost,* ed. Alastair Fowler (London: Longmans, 1974), Book 4, lines 598–99, p. 230.

12. Isobel St. John Bliss, *Edward Young* (Boston: Twayne, 1969), p. 126.

13. Steele, *Spectator,* no. 419, ed. Bond, 3:570.

14. Chalmers, *Works of the English Poets* 9:68; Kitty Scoular, *Natural Magic* (Oxford: Clarendon Press, 1965), pp. 81–117.

15. Davie, *Purity*, p. 49.

Chapter Six

1. Mitford, *Poetical Works of Parnell*, pp. 77–78.

2. Barnaby Barnes, in *Oxford Book of Sixteenth Century Verse* ed. E. K. Chambers, (Oxford: Clarendon Press, 1932), p. 431; Canticles, 3:1, 6:1; Francis Quarles, Emblem 3:7, *Complete Works*, ed. Alexander Grosart (New York: AMS Press, 1967); George Herbert, "The Search," line 1, *Works*, ed. F. E. Hutchinson (Oxford: Clarendon Press, 1941), p. 162; Nahum Tate, "The Search," *Poems Written on Several Occasions* (London, 1684); John Hughes in W. Duncombe, *The Works of Horace in English Verse* (London, 1767), 1:222.

3. *Miscellaneous Writings of John Evelyn*, ed. W. Upcott, (London, 1825), p. 537.

4. Vergil, *Georgics*, vol. 2, ll. 458–74.

5. The best treatment of this subject is by A. D. McKillop, *The Background of Thomson's "Seasons"* (Minneapolis: University Press, 1942).

6. See F. Cayré, *Manual of Patrology and History of Theology*, trans. H. Howitt (Tournai: Desclée & Co., 1936), 1:21.

7. R. D. Havens, "Parnell's 'Hymn to Contentment,' " *Modern Language Notes* 59 (1944):330.

8. H. H. Clark, "Melancholy in Edward Young," *Modern Language Notes* 39 (1924):129; P. van Tieghem, *La Poésie de la Nuit et des Tombeaux en Europe au XVIIIe Siècle* (Brussels: Academie Royale de Belgique, 1921).

9. H. G. De Maar, *History of Modern English Romanticism*, (Oxford: University Press, 1924), 1:183.

10. Amy L. Reed, *The Background of Gray's Elegy* (New York: Columbia University Press, 1924), pp. 25–26.

11. For comments on this tradition, brought to my attention by Graeme Watson, see *The Library of Drummond of Hawthornden*, ed. Robert H. MacDonald (Edinburgh: University Press, 1971), p. 30.

12. E. Arwaker, *The Birth-Night* (1705), cited by J. W. Draper, *The Funeral Elegy and the Rise of English Romanticism* (New York: University Press, 1929), p. 259.

13. Louis Martz, *The Poetry of Meditation* (New Haven: Yale University Press, 1954), p. 135.

14. Though Draper exaggerates the influence of these Puritan elegies, he provides a useful survey of them and other cognate poems.

15. Thomas Flatman, *Minor Poets of the Caroline Period*, ed. George Saintsbury (Oxford: Clarendon Press, 1921), 3:325; Nahum Tate, "Melancholy," *Poems Written on Several Occasions*, (London, 1684), p. 82.

16. William Hammond, *Minor Caroline Poets* ed. Saintsbury, 2:511; John Pomfret, *Supplement to the British Poets,* ed. Thomas Parks (London: J. Sharpe, 1808), 3:85–92; Bishop Ken, "Preparations for Death," cited in Draper, *The Funeral Elegy,* p. 277.

17. Thomas Sherlock's *Practical Discourse Concerning Death,* first published in 1681, reached a tenth edition in 1699.

18. Cf. Milton, "Il Penseroso," line 85.

19. Quarles, Emblem 2:1, *Complete Works,* 3:57; Marvell, *Last Instructions to a Painter,* lines 885–86, 916; *Richard III,* 5.3.179; William Congreve (1710), *The Mourning Bride, Poems and Miscellanies,* ed. Bonamy Dobrée, (Oxford: University Press, 1928), p. 290.

20. Isa. 34:11; Vergil, *Georgics,* 2:258; Dryden's *Aeneid,* 6, l. 427; *Titus Andronicus,* 2.3.97, 107; *Hamlet,* 3.2.444; Cowley's "The Complaint," l. 4.

21. William Drummond of Hawthornden, *Flowres of Sion,* 25, "Death's Last Will," *Poetical Works,* ed. L. E. Kastner, (Manchester: University Press, 1913), 2:32.

22. Peake, *Poetry of the Landscape and the Night,* p. 18.

23. Goldsmith, *Works,* "The Beauties of English Poetry," 5:325.

24. Fairchild, *Religious Trends* 1:236.

25. Ibid., p. 235.

26. A. P. Hudson, "The Hermit and Divine Providence," *Studies in Philology* 28(1931):218–34.

27. Ibid., p. 229.

28. London, 1702; translated by E. Law and published in 1731 (London).

29. *Spectator,* ed. Bond, 2:421. Several essays in *The British Mercury,* 28 January 1712, 1 and 4 February 1712, deal with the topic too. See also Voltaire's *Zadig,* ed. G. Ascoli (Paris: M. Didier, 1962), 2:136–44.

30. Boswell's *Johnson* 3:392.

31. Hudson, "The Hermit and Divine Providence," p. 232.

32. Ibid., pp. 222–23.

33. Cowley *Poems,* ed. Waller, p. 304.

34. Tertullian, *Adversus Marcionem,* cited F. Boas and A. O. Lovejoy, *Essays in Primitivism and Related Ideas in the Middle Ages* (Baltimore: Johns Hopkins Press, 1948), p. 90; Boethius, Metrum 6; Milton, especially *Paradise Regained* 3, ll. 186–87.

Chapter Seven

1. For a good brief account see Chester Chapin, *Personification in Eighteenth Century English Poetry* (New York: King's Crown Press, 1955). Another useful survey is P. K. Elkin's unpublished B. Litt. thesis, "The Attitude to Allegory in Poetry, 1660–1715," (Oxford, 1949).

2. Preface to *Prince Arthur: An Heroic Poem* (London, 1695).

3. *Spectator,* no. 419, ed. Bond, 3:570.

4. *The Iliad of Homer,* Books 1–9: Twickenham edition, *Poems of Alexander Pope* 7:6.

5. Crane, "On Writing the History of Criticism," *The Idea of the Humanities* (Chicago, 1967).

6. *Works of Spenser* (London, 1715), 1:lvi–lvii, cited by Earl Wasserman in "The Inherent Values of Eighteenth-Century Personification," *PMLA* 65 (1950):439.

7. Wasserman, *PMLA,* 65:435–63.

8. *Spectator,* ed. Bond, 4:122.

9. Ibid., p. 124.

10. Ibid., p. 278.

11. *The Tatler and the Guardian Complete in One Volume* (Edinburgh, 1880), p. 88; Richard Flecknoe, *Enigmaticall Characters* (London, 1658), p. 30.

12. *Tatler and Guardian,* p. 104.

13. The prose visions appear at the end of Pope's edition.

14. Swift's *Battle* was first published in 1704.

15. Pope's *Iliad,* 7:24.

16. Ibid., 7:lxxx.

17. Pope, *Correspondence,* 1:226–27.

18. Pope's *Iliad,* 7:lxxxi.

19. Anthony Collins, *A Discourse of Free Thinking* (London, 1713), p. 9.

20. Pope's *Iliad,* 7:29.

21. Donald Foerster, *Homer in English Criticism: The Historical Approach in the Eighteenth Century* (New Haven: Yale University Press, 1947), p. 28.

22. Pope's *Iliad,* 7:51–52.

23. Thomas Rhymer, *A Short View of Tragedy* (London, 1693), p. 45; John Dennis, *Critical Works,* ed. E. N. Hooker (Baltimore: John Hopkins Press, 1943), 2:337; *Spectator,* ed. Bond, 2:221, 315.

24. Pope's *Iliad,* 7:64, 68.

25. Ibid., p. lxxxii; Spence, *Anecdotes,* ed. Osborn, 1:84.

26. Pope's *Iliad,* 7:65.

27. Goldsmith, *Works: Life of Parnell,* 3:416.

28. Charles Kerby-Miller, *Memoirs of Scriblerus,* p. 29.

29. Swift, *Correspondence* 2:162–63.

30. Robert Steensma, *Dr. John Arbuthnot* (Boston: Twayne, 1979), p. 85.

31. Pope and Swift, *Miscellanies in Prose and Verse* (London, 1732), 3:368.

32. Pope, *Correspondence*, 1:333.

33. Pope, *Correspondence*, 1:395, 415.

34. Dircks, "Parnell's 'Batrachomuomachia.' "

35. The most convenient edition for the *Life and Remarks of Zoilus* would appear to be *The Poetical Works of Thomas Parnell*, ed. Rev. John Mitford. This quotation is from p. 131; hereafter page numbers cited in parentheses in the text. On *hypsos* see Pat Rogers, "Ironside Day by Day," *Times Literary Supplement*, 14 October 1983, p. 1115.

36. Sir J. E. Sandys, *A History of Classical Scholarship*, 3d ed. (Cambridge: University Press, 1921), 1:108–9.

37. *Pastoral Poetry and An Essay on Criticism*, ed. E. Audra and A. Williams (New Haven: Yale University Press, 1961), p. 292.

38. Sir William Temple, *A Short Account of Dr. Bentley's Humanity and Justice to those Authors who have written Before him* (London, 1699), pp. 92–93.

Chapter Eight

1. George Saintsbury, *A Short History of English Literature* (1898; London: Macmillan, 1913), p. 562.

2. F. R. Leavis, *Revaluation, Tradition and Development in English Poetry* (1936; Harmondsworth, England: Penguin, 1964), p. 94. Leavis adds that Parnell is of very minor interest but I hope it is not special pleading to point out that this must be seen in the light of the fact that Parnell is one of only five poets of the period that he regards as worth mentioning at all.

3. Reuben Brower, "Dryden and the Invention of Pope," *Restoration and Eighteenth-Century Literature, Essays in Honour of A. D. McKillop* (Chicago: University Press, 1963), p. 212.

4. *The London Magazine or Gentleman's Monthly Intelligencer* (June 1770), p. 319.

5. W. J. Courthope, *A History of English Poetry* (London, Macmillan, 1905), 5:190.

6. *Johnsonian Miscellanies*, ed. G. Birkbeck Hill, (Oxford: Clarendon Press, 1897), 2:428.

7. Joseph Warton, *Essay on the Genius and Writings of Pope*, vol. 1, 1756; vol. 2, 1782 (5th ed., 1806), p. vii.

8. Swift, *Stella*, p. 646; Aitken, *Life of Steele* (1889), 1:371.

9. Pope, 1717, *Correspondence* 1:396.

10. David Hume, "Of Simplicity and Refinement in Writing," *Essays*, ed. Green and Grose.

11. R. D. Havens, "Simplicity, a Changing Concept," *Journal of the History of Ideas* 14 (1953):3–32.

12. Joseph Spence, 1732, "The First History of English Poetry," *Pope and his Contemporaries: Essays presented to George Sherburn,* ed. James Osborn (Oxford: Clarendon Press, 1949), p. 250.

13. Hume, "Of Simplicity," *Essays,* pp. 240, 243.

14. William Shenstone, *Poems on Several Occasions* (Oxford, 1737), p. 56.

15. See Charles Lamb, 1 June 1796, *Letters of Charles and Mary Lamb,* ed. E. V. Lucas, (London: Dent and Methuen, 1935), I:7. See too Hamilton's poem "Contemplation, or The Triumph of Love." For Clare see Robert Protherough's unpublished B. Litt. thesis, "A Critical Study of John Clare's Poetry with Particular Reference to the Influence of Books and Authors on his Style" (Oxford, 1955), p. 199.

16. *The Poems of Thomas Gray, William Collins and Oliver Goldsmith,* ed. Roger Lonsdale (London: Longmans, 1969), ll. 77–78, 113–20, pp. 712–14; hereafter cited as Lonsdale, *Poems of . . . Goldsmith.*

17. "A City Night Piece" was published in no. IV, *The Bee,* 27 Oct. 1759, Goldsmith, *Works* 1:431. It contains several verbal echoes from Parnell.

18. Lonsdale, *Poems of . . . Goldsmith,* pp. 591, 598. The revelation of Angelina is like the transformation scene in "The Hermit."

19. Goldsmith, *Works,* vol. 3.

20. Lines 216–17 echo "Health" (p. 76). See T. Woodman, *Notes and Queries* 17 (August 1970):300.

21. Davie, *Purity of Diction,* pp. 14–15.

22. 23 April 1775, Boswell's *Johnson* 3:122, n2.

23. *Johnsonian Miscellanies* 2:255.

24. The first has no ascription of place, and is preceded by a text, John 7:13; the second was published in London, printed by M. Lewis.

25. John Wesley, *A Collection of Moral and Sacred Poems . . .* (London, 1744).

26. Boswell's *Johnson* 4:54.

27. Goldsmith, "An Enquiry into the Present State of Polite Learning in Europe," *Works* 1:319.

28. Lonsdale, *Poems of . . . Goldsmith,* p. 695.

29. Lane Cooper, "The Forest Hermit in Coleridge and Wordsworth," *Modern Language Notes* 24 (1909):33–36.

30. Richard Savage, "The Wanderer," canto 5, ll. 701–8. See too canto 2, l.5.

31. W. J. Courthope, *A History of English Poetry* (London: Macmillan, 1905), has a good account of Parnell's influence on Savage (5:192).

32. James Kinsley, *The Poems and Songs of Robert Burns* (Oxford: Clarendon Press, 1968), 1:233, ll.31–34; Aitken, Parnell's *Works,* p. 100.

33. Samuel Jackson Pratt also wrote under the name Courtney Melmoth. The poem is to be found in *Pity's Gift: A Collection of Interesting Tales from the Writings of Mr. Pratt, Selected by a Lady* (London, 1798), p. 19.

34. *Beauties of the Muses* . . . (Worcester, England, 1793).

35. Goldsmith, *Works* 3:426.

36. John Young, *Criticism on the Elegy Written in a Country Church-Yard,* (Edinburgh, 1810), 2d ed., p. 41.

37. *Broome's Poetical Works* ed. C. Cooke (London, 1796), p. 44; *Gentleman's Magazine* 15 (1745):661; 18 (1748):5, 6, 7.

38. Chalmers, 15:68. See also ll.60–62.

39. *Meditations Among the Tombs,* reprinted in *Meditations and Contemplations* (London: J. Smith, 18——), p. 49, n3; Walter Thomas, *Le Poète Edward Young* (Paris: Libraire Hachette, 1901), p. 368.

40. Peake, *Poetry of the Landscape and the Night,* p. 18.

41. Huizinga, *The Waning of the Middle Ages* (London: Edward Arnold, 1955), chap. 11.

42. See H. W. Starr, "Gray's Opinion of Parnell," *Modern Language Notes* 67 (1942):675–76.

43. Lonsdale, *Poems of Thomas Gray,* ll. 13–16, p. 120.

44. Davie, *Purity of Diction,* pp. 197–98.

45. See, for example, "To Content" by Anna Barbauld; "To Content" by Robert Cheetham; "Contentment" by Stephen Duck.

46. Fairchild, *Religious Trends* 1:236.

47. M. B. and L. M. Price, *The Publication of English Literature in Germany in the Eighteenth Century* (Berkeley: University of California Press, 1934), p. 393.

48. Abbé Yart, *Idée de la Poésie Anglaise,* vol. 5 (1754).

49. Van Tieghem, *La Poésie de la Nuit et des Tombeaux,* p. 12. Giovio also cites Parnell, and the Swiss poet Bridel imitated him.

50. 1774, Boswell's *Johnson* 5:433–34.

51. William Barron, *A Synopsis of Lectures on Belles Lettres and Logic,* 2d ed. (Edinburgh, 1770), p. 143.

52. Hugh Blair, *Lectures on Rhetoric and Belles Lettres* (London, 1783), 2:375.

53. Goldsmith, *Works* 3:422.

54. Leslie Stephen, *Hours in a Library,* 3d ser. (London: Smith, Elder & Co., 1879), pp. 175–76.

55. R. L. and Maria Edgeworth, *Readings on Poetry* (London, 1816).

56. Thomas Campbell, *Specimens of the British Poets* (1819; London: John Murray, 1844), p. 323.

57. Ibid., p. 86.

58. 1815, Wordsworth, "Essays Supplementary to the Preface," *Poems* (1815); *Wordsworth's Literary Criticism* ed. W. J. B. Owen (London: Routledge & Kegan Paul, 1974), p. 203.

59. See Earl Wasserman, *Modern Language Notes* 55 (1940):432–33.

60. 1827, "Specimens of a Dictionary of Love and Beauty," *New Monthly Magazine* 75:266–71. Attributed to Leigh Hunt by Louis Landre, *Leigh Hunt* (Paris: Editions Belleslettres, 1936), 2:493.

61. *The Album*, 1822, no. 2 (July), pp. 183–234.

62. William Hazlitt, *Select British Poets* (London: Thomas Flagg, 1825), p. xii. *Lectures on the English Poets and the Spirit of the Age*, ed. C. M. Maclean (New York: Dutton, 1967), pp. 104, 347.

63. Sir Samuel Egerton Brydges, *Gnomica* (Geneva, 1824), p. 175.

64. "The Hermit," "A Night Piece," "A Hymn to Contentment," and "A Fairy Tale" in particular.

65. C. H. Timperley, *Dictionary of Printers and Printing* (1839; 2d ed., London: H. Johnson, 1842), p. 670.

66. James Prior, *The Life of Oliver Goldsmith* (London: John Murray, 1837), 2:287.

67. *The Hermit*, ed. Thomas Kirk (London: Bemrose, 1874).

68. *Quarterly Review* 153 (1882):422.

69. E. K. Chambers, *The Bookman*, 6 (July, 1894):115–16.

70. W. B. Yeats, *A Book of Irish Verse* (London: Methuen, 1895), p. xiii.

71. Saintsbury, *A Short History of English Literature;* Gosse, *A History of Eighteenth Century Literature* (London: Macmillan, 1889), p. 137; Myra Reynolds, *The Treatment of Nature in English Poetry Between Pope and Wordsworth* (Chicago: University Press, 1896), p. 22.

72. *The English Poets*, ed. T. H. Ward (2d ed., London: Macmillan), 3:133–34; Gosse, *History of Eighteenth Century Literature*, pp. 136–37.

73. *All the Year Round, A Weekly Journal*, conducted by Charles Dickens, no. 197, 3d ser., (8 Oct. 1892), p. 343.

74. Hugh de l'Anson Fausset, *Minor Poets of the Eighteenth Century, Parnell, Green, Dyer and Anne, Countess of Winchelsea* (London: Dent, 1930).

75. *Poems of Thomas Parnell* (Dublin: Cuala Press, 1927).

76. A. H. Cruikshank. "Thomas Parnell, or What was Wrong with the Eighteenth Century?" *Essays and Studies* 7:57–81.

77. R. Wyse Jackson, "Thomas Parnell the Poet," *Dublin Magazine* 20:28–35.

78. Fairchild, *Religious Trends* 1:231–36.

79. Bonamy Dobrée, *English Literature in the Early Eighteenth Century, 1700–1740* (Oxford: Clarendon Press, 1959), p. 151; James Sutherland, *A Preface to Eighteenth Century Poetry*, p. 26.

80. Davie, *Purity of Diction*, pp. 26, 27.

Selected Bibliography

PRIMARY SOURCES

1. Individual Works

An Essay on the Different Styles of Poetry. London: B. Tooke, 1713. Reprinted in *Different Styles of Poetry: Irish Writings from the Age of Swift.* Edited by Robert Mahoney. Dublin: Cadenus Press, 1978.

"Essay on the Life, Writings and Learning of Homer." *The Iliad of Homer. Translated by Alexander Pope.* London: Lintot, 1715.

Homer's 'Battle of the Frogs and Mice,' with the Remarks of Zoilus, to which is Prefixd the Life of Zoilus. London: B. Lintot, 1717.

2. Collected Editions

Poems on Several Occasions, Written by Dr. Thomas Parnell. Edited by Alexander Pope. London: Lintot, 1722.

Works in Verse and Prose. Glasgow: Foulis, 1755. Contains authenticated variations on Pope's text.

The Posthumous Works of Dr. Thomas Parnell, Containing Poems Moral and Divine, and on Various Other Subjects. London: B. Gunne, 1758.

Works of the English Poets. Edited by Alexander Chalmers. Vol. 9. London: C. Whittingham, 1810.

The Poetical Works of Thomas Parnell. Edited by the Reverend John Mitford. Aldine Edition. London: Bell, 1833.

The Poetical Works of Thomas Parnell. Edited by George Aitken. Aldine edition. London: Bell, 1894.

Poems of Thomas Parnell. Edited by Lennox Robinson. Dublin: Cuala Press, 1927.

Minor Poets of the Eighteenth Century. Edited by Hugh de l'Anson Fausset. London: Dent, 1930.

3. Manuscripts

Various as yet unpublished poems, including several satires, elegies, songs, and imitations, are being prepared for the definitive edition by C. J. Rawson and F. P. Lock. For a survey description of this material see C. J. Rawson, "New Parnell Manuscripts," *Scriblerian* 1, no. 2 (Spring 1969):1–2.

SECONDARY SOURCES

1. Books and Articles

Cruikshank, A. H. "Thomas Parnell, or What was Wrong with the Eighteenth Century?" *Essays and Studies* 7, (1927):57–81. Despite its title this is an essay with some valuable points on, for example, Pope's revisions, and it ends with the plea that the poet be read again.

Davie, Donald. *Purity of Diction in English Verse.* New York: Oxford University Press, 1953. Makes a few brillilant critical comments on Parnell, and explains the whole context of "Purity of diction."

Dircks, Richard. "Parnell's 'Batrachomuomachia' and the Homer Translation Controversy." *Notes and Queries* 201 (1956):339–42. Sets the work in context.

Fairchild, Hoxie Neale. *Religious Trends in English Poetry.* New York: Columbia University Press, 1939, 1:231–36. An account of high Anglican traits in Parnell's religious verse, and a valuable differentiation between Parnell and later sentimental poets.

Goldsmith, Oliver. *Life of Parnell.* London: T. Davies, 1770. An interesting and reasonably accurate account of Parnell's life and a critical manifesto for his poetry against Gray in particular.

Havens, R. D. "Parnell's 'Hymn to Contentment.' " *Modern Language Notes* 59 (1944):329–31. A claim that the hymn is confused between contentment and bliss and a comment on Addison's influence.

Hudson, A. P. "The Hermit and Divine Providence." *Studies in Philology* 28 (1931):218–34. A very valuable study of analogues to Parnell's poem which shows how the poet refines on his source material.

Jackson, R. Wyse. "Thomas Parnell the Poet." *Dublin Magazine* 20 (1945):28–35. A short survey of the poet's achievement, especially praising "A Night Piece."

Rawson, C. J. "New Parnell Manuscripts." *Scriblerian* 1 (1969):1–2. See Primary Sources.

———. "Swift's Certificate to Parnell's Posthumous Works." *Modern Language Review* 57 (1962):179–82. Proves the authenticity of the *Posthumous Works.*

———, with F. P. Lock. "Scriblerian Epigrams by Thomas Parnell." *Review of English Studies* 33 (1982):148–57. Describes twelve manuscript epigrams.

Woodman, T. "Parnell, Politeness and 'Pre-Romanticism'." *Essays in Criticism* 33 (1983):205–19.

2. Theses

Martin, Mabel. "The Life and Works of Thomas Parnell." B. Litt. thesis,
    University of Oxford, 1930. Packed with helpful information, tran-
    scripts of letters, etc.
Schoedinger, P. S. "The Life and Works of Thomas Parnell." Ph. D.
    diss., Yale University, 1940. Valuable corrections of mistakes in
    previous accounts of the life. Reprints Parnell juvenilia in an appen-
    dix. Little critical insight into the poet, but indispensable.

Index

Vida, Marco G., 30

Waller, Edmund, 1, 17
Walsh, William, 38
Wanderer, The, 105–106
Warburton, William, 93
Warton, Joseph, 1, 101, 110
Warton, Thomas, 1, 102
Watts, Isaac, 15, 16, 20, 21
Wesley, John, 104

Winchelsea, Anne Finch, Lady, 67, 69, 71, 111
Wordsworth, William, 105, 111
Works of the Unlearned, The, 6

Yart, l'abbé Antoine, 109
Yeats, William Butler, 113
Young, Edward, 76, 107, 110
Young, John, 106

Zoilus, of Amphipolis, 97